Guided Writing

Practical Lessons, Powerful Results

Lori D. Oczkus

HEINEMANN
Portsmouth, NH

KH

Heinemann
A division of Reed Elsevier Inc.
361 Hanover Street
Portsmouth, NH 03801–3912
www.heinemann.com

Offices and agents throughout the world

The author and publisher wish to thank those who have generously given permission to reprint borrowed material:

"Strip Poem" from *Super Six Comprehension Strategies* by Lori Oczkus. Copyright © 2004. Published by Christopher-Gordon Publishers. Reprinted by permission of the publisher.

"Chart" from *Wondrous Words* by Katie Wood Ray. Copyright © 1999 by the National Council of Teachers of English. Reprinted with permission.

Library of Congress Cataloging-in-Publication Data
Oczkus, Lori D.
    Guided writing : practical lessons, powerful results / Lori D. Oczkus.
        p. cm.
    Includes bibliographical references.
    ISBN-13: 978-0-325-01071-7 (alk. paper)
    ISBN-10: 0-325-01071-4
    1. English language—Composition and exercises—Study and teaching (Elementary).   I. Title.
    LB1576.O298 2007
    372.62'3—dc22

                                                                    2006039843

Editor: Leigh Peake
Production: Abigail M. Heim
Typesetter: House of Equations, Inc.
Interior and cover design: Joyce Weston Design
Cover photography: Lawrence Migdale/PIX
Manufacturing: Jamie Carter

Printed in the United States of America on acid-free paper

11   10   09   08   07   EB   2   3   4   5

2/7/08

Contents

Appendices

Acknowledgments

I would like first to express heartfelt thanks to the hundreds of teachers and students in California and across the country who allow me into their schools to teach and grow alongside them. While in these busy classrooms I learn about the craft and realities of scaffolding writing instruction. The sometimes brutal honesty of both teachers and students moves my teaching forward. I decided to write this book to honor them.

When I ask students which of them enjoys writing, often only a few hands go up. Sometimes I also ask them to define writing in their own words. They respond with comments like:

Writing is putting your ideas on paper.

Writing is expressing yourself.

Writing is communicating with others.

Their definitions provide a window into their attitudes toward writing. Sometimes evidence of our emphasis on testing is blatant. One child raised her hand when I asked, "What is writing?" and rattled off the three genres on the district writing proficiency including response to literature, summary, and personal narrative. Another child, a fifth grader, wondered whatever happened to writing about topics of choice and writers workshop. Students often admit that writing isn't fun any more.

After working in many classrooms and listening to teachers and students complain about writing, I decided my goal for this text would be to provide practical lessons that improve writing and motivate students to enjoy writing. I am especially grateful to the staffs at the California elementary schools of Del Rey, Randall, Sinnott, Washington, Wilson, and Lincoln for allowing me to work in their schools while developing these lessons. Special thanks go to Robyn Arthur, Margie Musante, Jill Hope, Kim Burris, Terry Brash, Judy Puckett, Sandy Buscheck, Kelly Thrane, Elisa Carpenter, Katy Johnson, Carol Levin, Kristin Choy, Gery Baura, Kathy Murray, Karen Berry, Kathy McPherrin, and Judy Herns.

Also, I need to express gratitude to my little band of readers: Audrey Fong, Carla Hoff, and Ellen Osmundson—their feedback kept me on track as I wrote this book. Special thanks to Lois Bridges for encouraging my ideas and writing style. Heartfelt thanks to Regie Routman and Linda Hoyt for their insightful books and supportive advice.

Team Heinemann deserves a round of applause for their extreme dedication to providing the very best books possible for teachers. Leigh Peake, thanks for your constant support, persistence, and professionalism.

At home I owe thanks to my own little group of writers: Bryan, a freshman in high school; Rachael, a seventh grader; and Rebecca, a third grader. I learn every day from them about the challenges and joys of writing. Thanks to my husband, Mark, whose love, support, and cooking kept me going while writing. Thanks also to my parents, Bruce and Barbara Dutton, who always believed I could write.

Introduction

Writing is fun and makes people smile. I like writing because it feels like magic
    —Alayna

Writing in the Old Days . . .

What do you remember about learning to write in school? Perhaps your early writing experiences were much like mine. Dull. I distinctly recall writing in sixth grade. The lessons followed a predictable pattern. Mrs. Evans gave an assignment and then instructed, "Get out your pencils and write for the next twenty minutes." The stuffy, stifling room grew silent except for the annoying grind of the pencil sharpener as four or five reluctant writers tried to buy a bit more time. There was no modeling, no working together to brainstorm ideas, no rich word bank on the board, and no peer editing or revising. The only sharing of our work came when Mrs. Evans read or asked a student to read the occasional piece of exemplary writing.

When I began teaching, I didn't want to inflict the boring writing environment I had experienced as a child on my students. I couldn't wait to make writing instruction meaningful and fun. My goal has always been to motivate students to write well and to feel like writers. And in the past twenty years we *have* come a long way in our writing instruction. Now we support writers through prewriting, drafting, editing, and creating final copies that we share. We model how to write; we think aloud in front of our students; we draw concrete examples from literature and student work. We even support writers by composing together in shared and interactive writing. In writing workshop, writers explore topics of their choice and work with us and their peers to improve their craft. We provide rubrics with clear expectations for writing assignments. Traits of good writing, including ideas, organization, voice, sentence fluency, and conventions, guide our lessons and assessments.

The Pressure Is On!

Yet even with all this support, students often still stare at the intimidating blank page and teaching writing is still a challenge. The specter of state and national standards and testing add to the pressure that we feel to improve student writing. The National Assessment of Educational Progress (NAEP), or the Nation's Report Card as it is often referred to, confirms there is growing concern about student writing: many of our students, sometimes up to two-thirds, are performing below proficient standards.

Rigorous state tests can be difficult for students to pass as well. One fourth-grade teacher friend of mine adds, "I work hard teaching writing, and the students do show progress, but the tests don't always reflect what my students can write. I am really frustrated."

In my work as a literacy consultant in schools around the country I find that many teachers share my concern about teaching writing:

My students write dull, listy pieces and don't add details about their topics.

The students have difficulty organizing their ideas.

I model writing, and then when students write their own pieces they miss parts of the assignment.

Voice is missing from my student's work. They write such dull stories.

Report writing is getting harder for them. They have difficulty synthesizing information and organizing their ideas.

During writing workshop I have trouble meeting with all my students. I can only confer with a few.

With all the district and state writing assessments we have to give, I have given up allowing students to choose their topics in writing. We simply don't have the time. Help!

We are so focused on teaching the writing genres that are on the test that we have lost our joy for teaching writing.

Sound familiar?

Guided Writing—The Missing Piece

How can we meet the demand for better writing and improved test scores while putting joy back into our teaching? What best practices will improve student writ-

ing? For a while I focused heavily on modeled writing, thinking that was the answer. I wrote in front of students on projected transparencies and on chart paper. I followed my modeling with shared writing, in which we wrote a piece together. Even though this approach yielded much better results, students often still missed the mark. I needed more ways to support their writing development. Something was missing.

In my search for better writing instruction, I began to think about the scaffolded way in which we teach reading: modeling by thinking aloud, engaging students in shared reading, guiding students in cooperative or teacher-led groups, and finally encouraging students to work independently. During my writing instruction I was modeling up a storm and doing some shared writing, but I wasn't doing enough guided writing. I began to play with the idea of adding a "middle piece"—supported, or guided, writing—before releasing students to write independently. Along the way I had many questions:

- What exactly is guided writing?

- Is guided writing parallel to guided reading?

- Is guided writing always done with small groups?

- Can I guide writing in whole-class lessons using cooperative learning?

- How will taking the time to use guided writing improve student writing?

- What do guided writing lessons look like with different genres and at different grade levels?

- What are some creative and motivational ways to make students feel supported as they write?

- How will I make time for one more piece of instruction in my already busy schedule?

- How often should I make use of guided writing strategies?

As I searched for answers, I didn't find many resources on guided writing. While the teachers I chatted with bobbed their heads yes, they knew what guided writing was, their definitions varied. I found a few, but only a few, articles and chapters in professional books devoted to the topic of guided writing. So I set out to build on scaffolded learning research and what we know about good writing instruction and find a way to make guided writing an effective component in my writing program.

What Does Guided Writing Look Like in the Classroom?

During the next seven years, the teachers with whom I worked and I continued to teach whole-class lessons but added a guided writing step, using it at a variety of grade levels. Here are just a few of the things we did:

- After reading an article about the sinking of the *Titanic*, fifth graders worked on group reports while I moved from table to table supporting and guiding their work. They scored one another's group reports before writing their individual reports on one of our nation's fifty states.

- Small groups of third graders wrote guided narratives about a roller-coaster ride after I had modeled how to write a narrative. Then individual students wrote their stories on a special form that guided their writing.

- Groups of first graders worked together writing different beginnings to the same story, then shared their work with the whole class on projected transparencies. During writing workshop, each student used one of the suggested beginnings to start her or his own piece.

- A group of second-language students from all grade levels combined individual "noisy" observations into a group poem. Then each student wrote his or her own poem, incorporating what had been learned about bringing voice into one's writing. (Later, poetry began showing up everywhere, even in daily journals!)

We consistently found that as a result of these guided writing experiences student writing and motivation improved dramatically.

Guided writing is now a staple in my bag of writing tools. In this book, I share a practical model for guiding your students to improve all aspects of their writing. Specifically, you'll find:

- definitions of guided writing, along with classroom examples/vignettes from a variety of grade levels

- ways guided writing fits into an overall scaffolded writing program that includes modeled, shared, guided, and independent writing

- engaging, practical lessons that motivate students to write better and love writing

- lessons organized around the whole class, cooperative writing groups, and teacher-led small groups

- creative ways for using the lessons during writing workshop or guided reading

- practical suggestions, in every lesson, for incorporating "six-trait writing" (ideas, organization, voice, sentence fluency, word choice, and conventions), an approach to teaching writing originated by Vicki Spandel, Ruth Culham, and the Northwest Educational Laboratory

- reproducibles to use in the classroom

- student examples

- suggestions for small-group conferences

- rubrics for helping students assess their own work

- staff development and coaching suggestions.

How to Read This Book

I write books for busy teachers. Therefore, this is a "flippy" book. You can skip or flip around in the lessons and chapters, picking and choosing what your students need to succeed. However, it will be helpful to get the big picture of how I have uniquely defined guided writing in Chapters 1 and 2. The purpose of those chapters is to give you a broad overview of guided writing within the context of specific steps that apply to any grade level or genre. By reading Chapters 1 and 2 first, you'll see how guided writing might work for you and discover ways to implement it immediately. The other chapters are rich resources for applying guided writing to genres ranging from reports to poetry. Feel free to pick and choose from the lessons in these chapters in any order that makes sense for your students. (If you are a literacy coach, this book is also designed for group study.)

Each genre chapter includes the following features:

- an overview of the lesson concept and the rationale for the lesson

- stories that show guided writing in action in both primary and intermediate classrooms

- specific steps for scaffolding the lesson by way of modeled, shared, and especially guided writing before allowing students to write on their own

- published fiction or nonfiction to use in connection with the identifying examples/modeling portion of the lesson (when appropriate)

- suggestions for using the lesson during writing workshop, in whole-class lessons, and in small-group instruction (to include working with students who struggle with writing)

- graphic organizers and other reproducibles to use in guiding the lesson

- "cool tools" (overhead transparencies, sticky notes, butcher paper, sentence strips, markers, highlighters) for students to use in guided writing groups

- ways to incorporate the "six traits" in teaching and assessing writing

- rubrics for students to use as they write their own pieces and for you to use in guided small-group conferences

- questions for roundtable discussions, staff development sessions, or individual study.

Chapter by Chapter

- *Chapter 1, Scaffolding Writing Instruction: Guiding Writers:* This chapter provides some popular definitions of guided writing in the context of a unique spin that can be applied in a variety of settings in both primary and intermediate grades. It addresses these issues:

  - Is guided writing parallel to guided reading? (Just so you won't worry, it isn't!)

  - What are the benefits of guided writing for students and teachers?

  - How does research support guided writing?

  - How often should I use guided writing?

  - How does guided writing fit into my already busy writing curriculum?

  - What does guided writing look like in the classroom?

  In addition, it outlines the steps for scaffolding writing and provides two exciting lessons, one on descriptive writing, the other on responding to literature through poetry.

- *Chapter 2, Using Scaffolded Writing Steps, Cool Tools, and Graphic Organizers:* This chapter provides detailed descriptions of what modeled, shared, guided, and independent writing look like, as well as explanations of how to use guided writing during whole-class lessons, with cooperative groups, and with intervention groups. You'll also find ideas for using guided writing during writing workshop and guided reading and practical management tools to help you incorporate guided writing into your own writing program.

Chapter 3, Finding Your Voice: Noisy Poems: "Noisy words," or onomatopoeia, bring life to student writing. When they begin the year by writing free verse, students discover their voice naturally. Or you can use this type of poetry all year long. The result? Even reluctant writers write freely and with voice. The chapter includes exciting minilessons on word choice, descriptive language, and the effective use of metaphors and similes. Students choose their own topics and write away in groups and on their own. As a way to draw out your students' voices in their writing, this poetry really works!

Chapter 4, What's Your Story? Personal Narrative and Weekend Webs: Many schools ask students to record their weekend activities in a journal on Monday morning. Students usually write dull, "listy" pieces as they try to cover everything they did over the two days. In contrast, by brainstorming a weekend web, they cluster their weekend and then select one narrow event or topic to expand and elaborate on, writing about a slice of their life with flair and detail. Students love weekend webs because they help them uncover topics they care about. Weekend webs are a great way to incorporate student choice while building important writing skills.

Chapter 5, Write This Way! Patterned Writing, Text Structure, and Author's Craft:

When students study the textual patterns in fiction and nonfiction, first analyzing and then borrowing another author's organizational pattern or word choice, their writing improves. The structure provided allows students to free and celebrate their own writing voice. Groups of students write collaborative pieces to share and then work on individual pieces to collect in a class book. A class-created rubric is an effective way to conduct small-group conferences. These lessons help students think critically and read with a writer's eye!

Chapter 6, Read and Write All About It! Expository Writing: These lessons help students internalize the steps in writing an effective report: a good beginning, paragraphs that build and flow, and a strong ending. (Small-group intervention lessons for struggling writers are included.) First, the class, working in groups, composes reports that they then evaluate and score. Cool tools make the lesson fun, but the skills "stick." Finally, each student writes a report on her or his own.

Chapter 7, Lights, Camera, Action! Acting Out Narratives: Elementary students can enter a pretend world on a moment's notice. Vivian Paley's story plays allow them to do just that. You will be amazed at how quickly students, working in teams, compose these delightful little dramas that they then act out for one another. The modeling phase includes dramatizing sample story plays and composing a class story play. The chapter includes ideas for using this technique with older or younger buddies. Story plays bring students' writing alive in new and creative ways.

The *appendixes* are filled with tools for using guided writing in your classroom. The handy assessment rubrics guide your instruction as you work your way through the scaffolded writing model. Minilessons on response to literature, sentence elaboration, and characters representing the six writing traits provide quick, motivating ideas for improving writing. Ways for students to share writing such as the gallery tour or paper passing motivate students to revise their work. A list of children's books as well as professional resources on writing are also included.

I hope you will make these lessons your own and, in the process, discover that your students are enjoying themselves while improving their writing craft. Guided writing is a "best practice" that can make a difference. Happy writing!

Chapter One

Scaffolding Writing Instruction: Guiding Writers

Writing is a way of sharing your thoughts and creativity.
—Hannah

Why should we incorporate guided writing into our writing programs? How will it benefit students and make our teaching more effective? Guided writing is a flexible tool that *saves valuable time* by making our instruction crystal clear. Guided practice helps ensure that students really "get" what we are teaching the first time we introduce a writing skill or strategy.

Part of good scaffolding during any lesson involves guided practice. Before I incorporated guided writing into my teaching, my lessons didn't always include enough guided practice. I usually did a nice job of modeling and building a rubric or checklist for good writing, and then I jumped to having students write on their own.

I Modeled, They Wrote, But It Wasn't Enough

I remember the moment it struck me that I might need to add guided writing to strengthen my writing lessons. I was teaching a series of lessons in a third-grade classroom that I visited once or twice a week for three months. My goal was to teach the students to write stories and personal narratives. We were working on techniques for describing a setting. I modeled by writing about when I went scuba diving with my husband in Hawaii and a small (and harmless) four-foot-long shark trapped our group in a cave. (I also showed them an underwater photo of the shark.) Writing on a projected transparency as I thought aloud, I described my heart pounding, my "Darth Vader" breathing, and the bright little yellow tang fish darting around staring at me with black beady eyes. Then I asked the students to turn to a partner and discuss what they liked about my description. Finally, we built a list of criteria for a good setting description on the whiteboard that included sensory descriptions.

Then I asked the students to describe a time they were really scared. (It's always a good idea to select a common topic that they have all experienced.) They discussed their ideas with a partner, who asked questions about their setting. As I moved around the room conferring with individual students, I had to prompt many of them to shut their eyes and "see, hear, feel" the scene in their head and then find the words to describe it. For some, this additional one-on-one scaffolding was enough. Others were still stuck, searching both for ideas and the words to express them. What if I allowed them to practice writing a setting description in groups before I set them loose to write their own?

The next week I brought in my underwater description again. Partners turned to each other to review the criteria for writing a description. I invited some students to read their scary-situation descriptions aloud. I then grouped the students into teams and asked each team to write a descriptive piece about finding a coyote in their backyard (a recent problem in the neighborhood) as I moved from table to table offering guidance. Each team copied their descriptive writing onto an overhead transparency and shared it with the class. The rest of the class complimented the work and asked questions. This is what one team wrote:

Coyote Encounter in the Backyard

I saw flashing yellow eyes. I spotted its bushy, brownish-gray fur. Something slipped through the dark bushes into the cold night air. I lifted the sticky lid of the old garbage can. Two fierce, round, yellow eyes from deep inside the trash can stared up at me.

After everyone had shared, we returned to the criteria we'd created earlier and added the use of interesting verbs. This time when they went back to their individual pieces, the results were amazing. Their descriptions were detailed and full of voice:

Whee! Vroom! The roller coaster shot down the hill like a bullet. It slowed down a bit and I looked up. A lone seagull hovered in the blue sky high above me. The people above me on the roller coaster were screaming. I looked at the seat next to me and it had a big wad of gum stuck to it.
—Ryan

Then I saw it. That shiny red sign that read: The Blood Dripper. I froze. The line was like a ghost town with no one in it. I smelled buttery popcorn and yummy greasy hot dogs.
—Cecily

Thrilled with the results of my experiment, I began to look for interesting ways to sneak guided writing opportunities into my writing lessons at *all* grade levels. I wondered:

- What if I used guided writing during writing workshop even though the students are working on topics of their own choosing?

- How would guided writing look if I pulled together small temporary groups to work on the skills they needed?

- What if I incorporated some quick, guided writing techniques during guided reading to strengthen both comprehension and writing?

- How could I use guided writing during whole-class lessons but yet meet with just one small intervention or special-needs group, or even several temporary groups?

What Is Guided Writing?

Guided writing is a bridge between shared writing and independent writing, a scaffold that supports students with helpful tools as they move into writing on their own. The lessons may be conducted with the whole class, in small temporary groups, during guided reading, or during writing workshop. Specific settings include:

- whole-class lessons that incorporate cooperative learning and teacher conferences with individuals and small groups

- small temporary groups of students who need more practice in a genre or with a skill (groups may meet regularly or as needed)

- writing workshop, either in the minilesson or during conferences

- a quickwriting experience following guided reading in which students summarize or respond to the reading

Here are some additional definitions and explanations from leading teacher educators and literacy experts:

> The student is now in charge, holding the pen and attempting to apply what has been previously demonstrated and practiced with the direct support of the teacher and/or group. The students' guided practice is likely to be only as good as our demonstrations. . . . [S]tudents are encouraged to monitor their work and move toward independence. (Routman, *Writing Essentials*, 2005, pp. 71–72)

> Guided writing is an instructional approach where the teacher observes, prompts, and monitors the students during the act of writing, ensuring the skills and strategies learned in reading are applied to produce accurate, fluent, and expressive writing. . . . In process writing we have become used to whole-class minilessons followed by intensive supports at the assessment stage of the final product. Guided writing provides small-group guidance during drafting to support the entire process more effectively. (Mooney, "Guided Writing," in *Exploring Informational Texts*, 2003a, pp. 15, 119)

> In guided writing, you pull together small, temporary groups of writers and teach the craft, strategies, and skills those writers need at that particular time. (Fountas and Pinnell, *Guiding Readers and Writers*, 2001, p. 50)

Despite the variations in these definitions, there is consensus on one critical point: many students need more scaffolding or support while they are writing in order to produce quality pieces

Is Guided Writing Parallel to Guided Reading?

In her book *Writing Essentials* (2005), Regie Routman contends that "guided writing is *not* parallel to guided reading." I couldn't agree more. For one thing, if we suggested that teachers meet with small guided writing groups as often as they meet with their guided reading groups, they simply wouldn't do it. It would be wonderful if we could provide such targeted small-group instruction, but it would be a logistical nightmare. There aren't enough hours in a day to rotate through four or five small writing groups.

Guided writing is a flexible support tool to use with temporary (or cooperative) groups and during conferences. We need to look at all the options guided writing and guided practice offer and choose what works. Routman uses guided writing in small groups occasionally—when children are writing summaries or responses to literature, for example. Mostly, she suggests using guided writing as guided practice during whole-class lessons, along with peer conferences, whole-class sharing, and individual conferences. I usually incorporate the benefits of small-group instruction during my whole-class lessons by using cooperative learning and informal "table" groups. In other words, we can have our cake and eat it too: our students benefit from being pulled into small, guided groups during whole-class lessons, but we don't have to deal with managing and rotating formal groups every week as we do in reading.

I should add, however, that at Wilson School, a wonderful urban school in San Leandro, California, the first-grade teachers, instead of conducting a writing workshop, teach writing in small groups set up like their guided reading groups. The children who are not meeting with the teacher work at their tables on independent writing they began under the teacher's guidance. We need to keep in mind that there isn't one "right" way to do guided writing but that it is an excellent step for providing extra support. There are many options for whole-class groupings, writing workshop, and small-group instruction, so we can choose what is best for our students.

What Are the Benefits of Guided Writing?

Benefits to students that make guided writing worth the effort include:

- More modeling takes place, and there are more examples to "copy" and more ideas to incorporate into independent writing.

- Graphic organizers and other scaffolding tools help students move into independent writing.

- Students receive immediate teacher feedback.

- Students have more conferences with the teacher and their peers.

- Rubrics and other criteria set up clear expectations.

The Gradual-Release Learning Model

Teachers and students have multiple roles during the full spectrum of writing instruction. The teacher models, guides, coaches, and facilitates. The student observes, practices with the support of the teacher and peers, and tries the skill on his or her own while incorporating what has been learned.

The "gradual release" model of instruction (Fielding and Pearson 1991; Duke and Pearson 2002) suggests that we provide varying levels of support to students during a scaffolded lesson. Sports analogies are great ways to think about scaffolding our teaching. When a child is learning to play a sport, say baseball, he first watches others play the game. The coach demonstrates a technique, such as hitting the ball with a bat. Then the coach often stands next to the child and holds the child's hands on the bat, demonstrating and guiding as they practice swinging together. Finally, the coach allows the child to try hitting the ball on his or her own. During independent practice the coach verbally supports the child's attempts and offers advice on how to improve. At any point the coach might return to the guided step and take hold of the child's hands on the bat. When my son learned to play T-ball in second grade, the ball, rather than being pitched to the fledgling players, was placed on a stand directly in front of the batter. The stand was a scaffold until the children could hit the ball into the air.

During writing instruction we demonstrate by writing in front of the children while thinking aloud. We also help children identify elements of good writing by encouraging them to find examples of excellent writing in the literature they read. Just as in baseball, we "hold onto the bat," monitoring children during shared and guided writing lessons until they can write on their own. Like the baseball coach, we might support students by going back at any moment to guided practice. As the T-ball coach provides a ball stand as an intermediate tool, we might offer a graphic organizer, a pattern or technique borrowed from literature, or a rubric to guide students toward successful independent efforts. The teacher continues to alternate between a more supported guided step and independent practice. Each time a new or more sophisticated skill is added, the cycle repeats—model, guide, practice—with the teacher giving the appropriate support for each writer.

We can also use the learner's zone of proximal development (Vygotsky 1978) to help us understand guided writing. Vygotsky suggests that learners have a developmental level that is the "distance between the actual developmental level as determined by independent problem solving and the level of potential development as determined through problem solving under adult guidance or in collaboration with more capable peers" (p. 4). The broad guided writing model defined in this book offers many strategies for supporting students at their current developmental level: modeling, structuring assignments, coaching, relying on peers.

Learning is social, and the collaborative nature of guided writing provides a friendly and safe environment in which students can practice writing. All students benefit and grow from working in this type of cooperative setting. Most of the classrooms I work in are filled with English language learners, and research suggests they in particular need an interactive setting in order to thrive. In *When English Language Learners Write* (2006), Katherine Davies Samway says that for ELL students, "opportunities to talk about their writing, both while writing and at the end of a writing occasion, are invaluable" (p. 58). Teachers are always amazed at the difference the guided writing model makes in the quality of all their students' work.

A Classroom Example

To see how guided writing incorporates gradual release and the zone of proximal development, let's return to the vignette at the beginning of this chapter. As you recall, I was presenting a series of lessons to third graders on how to write stories. The entire sequence covered starting a story, writing interesting descriptions, setting up the problem, developing the action (instead of racing to a conclusion), and ending the story.

First we hunted in books for examples of good story beginnings. After we shared and discussed those, I wrote the beginning of my story about the shark, demonstrating my thought processes and acting out some of my choices. I started with the "noisy" word *splash* to convey jumping into the water wearing ten pounds of scuba gear and paddling my way around. Then I acted out "I am nervous" as I mimed stepping to the edge of the boat with the heavy scuba gear loaded on my back. After I wrote the first few sentences, I asked them to contribute to the next few.

Then, instead of turning the students loose and asking them to write their own story beginnings, I added a middle, guided step. I had students, in groups, write beginnings for a story about a coyote that had been rummaging through trash cans in the neighborhood. They shared their openings and we compared the various techniques. Then, using my shark story as a model, we discussed pointers for a good beginning and developed a checklist, or rubric. Finally the students worked independently as I conferred with them individually. The students also conducted small-group peer conferences using the rubric and our shared/modeled example as the standard.

For each subsequent lesson on other parts of story writing—developing the plot, solving the problem, ending the story—we followed the same pattern. We first searched classroom books to identify what it was we wanted to do as writers. Then I added to my shark story and invited their feedback. After that the students, in groups, added the new element to their coyote story. They shared their effort with the class, and we identified criteria for good writing that students then used to guide their work on their individual story.

Perhaps you're thinking, *didn't these step-by-step lessons take forever?* It did take a bit of extra time to weave in the guided step as I taught each element of story writing, but it was worth it because the quality of the students' writing improved. When we wrote stories later in the year, the students by and large no longer needed as much guided practice, although I did pull together a small group from time to time. We also continued to write shared stories together as a class as an alternate means of support.

Gradually withdrawing your support lets students reach their highest level of development. Constant teacher coaching and peer interactions support students as they move further along in their writing abilities. Most of all, students enjoy guided writing lessons because they have fun while learning!

How Often Should I Conduct Guided Writing Lessons?

Guided writing is a flexible tool that you can use whenever students need extra support to be successful (see Figure 1.1). Most likely you will not need to use a guided writing lesson for everything you teach; it's a tool you can apply when you need to.

Some teachers use guided writing when they begin teaching a new genre—poetry, reports, narratives, whatever. For example, fifth-grade teachers Robyn Arthur and Margie Musante, at Del Rey School, in Orinda, California, use guided report writing before they set students loose to write reports on their own. (I outline this process in detail in Chapter 6.)

Figure 1.1

Use Guided Writing to . . .

✎ introduce a new genre such as nonfiction or report writing or poetry

✎ teach a new skill such as writing a paragraph or a beginning or an ending

✎ reinforce reading and learn craft from the authors of fiction or nonfiction

---

During whole-class lessons, you might want to pull together a small group of children who need extra support and practice in the same skill—writing paragraphs, for example. Each student can contribute a sentence to the group paragraph, or each student can write a paragraph on his or her own and receive feedback from the group.

Another way to use guided writing during either whole-class lessons or writing workshop is to gather a group with similar needs while they compose their own pieces. For example, during a writing workshop in second grade, I noticed that five students were still struggling with prewriting after a shared writing lesson. I called these students to the rug up front and walked them through each step of brainstorming using a web, modeling as I went along. Then they talked with a partner about what they wanted to say, noting these things on their webs before they began writing. The small guided group provided just the support these writers needed to get going.

There are many ways to conduct small guided writing groups (see Figure 1.2). Some teachers, like the first-grade teachers at Wilson School, use small-group guided writing with all their students every week. Other teachers meet with one small writing group per day. Maybe this type of intensive regular small-group instruction appeals to you.

Or perhaps you will keep a small group together for a short time. When my fifth-grade cooperative groups were working together on report writing, I had the struggling writers work with me in a guided group for two weeks. The students learned to write a report, gained writing confidence, and received the intensive instruction they needed before writing on their own. Grateful parents stopped me in the grocery store and at school to thank me and couldn't believe the difference that the guided writing experience had made in their children's writing. The proof was in the independent reports that the struggling group wrote and in their scores on the district writing test.

Teacher and author Linda Hoyt (2003) suggests teaching guided writing *during* guided reading as a way of helping students read and write nonfiction. For example, she teaches the features of nonfiction text, such as words in boldface type, and then encourages students to write a brief piece and highlight the words they think are most important. When students write in front of her in the small group, she can coach them in their efforts. Another option Hoyt suggests is to follow the guided reading lesson with a writing workshop in which students incorporate the nonfiction features they've studied in texts into their own pieces.

Figure 1.2

Settings and Options for Guided Writing Instruction

✐ Use guided writing in table groups as needed during whole-class lessons or writing workshop. (*Model for the whole group, have table groups practice the skill, ask individuals to use the skill in their independent writing project.*)

✐ During whole-class lessons, assemble a temporary group that is struggling. (*Model for the whole group; as students work independently, pull together one group that needs support based on observations and writing samples.*)

✐ Use guided writing during guided reading. (*Model reading the material and writing a response, have students each respond to a portion of the text and combine their responses, or have each student write an independent piece while conferring with the group and teacher.*)

✐ Circulate among several guided writing groups. (*Model for the whole class, write a shared piece with the class, then create temporary groups based on shared needs as the students work on group and individual pieces.*)

Whatever approach you take, when you take the time to use guided writing, you can be assured that your students will truly internalize what you have taught.

How Does Guided Writing Relate to Six-Trait Writing?

Perhaps your school district is one of the thousands across the country that implement six-trait writing. These schools build their assessments and lessons around six traits that constitute good writing for writers of any age or in any genre:

1. *Ideas*: Writers first need to generate their own ideas to write about. Writers think about developing main ideas and details surrounding their ideas.

2. *Organization*: Good writers then work through a logical organization for their ideas as they develop and expand them. Organization includes writing a strong beginning and ending.

3. *Voice*: Every writer has a unique voice or personality that makes his or her writing special. Humor, personality, emotions, and the creative use of words bring a writer's voice alive. When writing has voice, it is much more engaging.

4. *Word choice*: Good writers choose interesting and exact words to relay their message. They vary their descriptive vocabulary and sometimes employ metaphors and similes to create rich visual images.

5. *Sentence fluency*: Interesting writing includes sentences that are varied in length, grammatical construction, and word choice.

6. *Conventions*: Conventions can make or break a writer. A slew of misspelled words and poor punctuation get in the way of even the best message. Good writers proofread, confer with others, and use reference tools to ensure they put their best foot forward.

These six traits are tools you may (or may not) decide to weave into any writing lesson. Guided writing lessons are the perfect place either to introduce a trait or to revise writing to incorporate a specific trait (see Appendix C). Here are some ways you might use guided writing and the six traits in your classroom:

✐ Gather a guided writing group that needs to work on one of the traits, such as organization. When writing reports, organizing one's notes, ideas, and information is often difficult for young writers. The small-group setting is ideal for honing in on this trait.

✐ You notice that your students' writing is stilted. Teach a minilesson to the whole class on using more colorful words or your emotional responses to the material to add voice to your writing and let them practice these techniques in guided writing groups.

✐ Group students at tables and move quickly from table to table presenting a five-minute lesson on sentence fluency. Have students read stories or nonfiction, searching for varied sentence beginnings, a common problem for young writers.

STEPS in a Scaffolded Writing Lesson

affolded lesson

Each step includes *optional* **cool tools**, or ways to engage students in the lesson and keep them thinking along the way. These tools also serve as informal assessments for deciding how much more practice and support your students will need.

Identifying Examples

Students study examples of the writing skill, strategy, or technique in books, articles, and even exemplary student work and list criteria that can serve as a rubric: *How to. . . .*

Cool Tools: highlight copies of pages from the text, mark pages, act out text.

Modeling

The teacher models and thinks aloud in front of the class or group on a chart or overhead. Students discuss what they observe about the writing and add to the rubric.

Cool Tools: thumbs-up or thumbs-down signals as teacher asks for feedback; writing suggestions on slates at their desks.

Shared Writing

The teacher works with the class and records the groups' writing suggestions. Or the teacher may call up a volunteer to write in front of the group. The teacher prompts the student as he or she writes. The class compliments the student and adds to the rubric.

Cool Tools: response signals.

The teacher asks, "Is this a good [whatever]?" and students show a thumbs-up or thumbs-down. Students may also write on slates at their desks.

Guided Writing

The teacher works with small groups who practice the writing. The teacher either rotates from table to table, briefly meeting with each, or gathers one group with similar needs. The group composes a joint piece with each writer contributing, or individual writers bring their independent writing to the group to discuss. They add criteria to the class rubric.

- ✐ *Guided writing during whole-class lessons or writing workshop.* The teacher rotates to cooperative table groups and confers with the group and with individuals.

- ✐ *Flexible guided writing group.* The teacher may gather a small, temporary group to work together based on need.

- ✐ *Guided writing during guided reading.* After reading in a small group, the teacher models writing in response to the reading and guides students in doing so. Writing may carry over to writing workshop.

Cool Tools: sentence strips, sticky notes, adding-machine tape, overhead transparencies, butcher paper.

Independent Writing

Students use the class-created rubric as a guide and write independently.

Cool Tools: a bookmark containing a rubric (or a similar personal reference).

Guided Conferring

Students meet with the teacher and/or peers to discuss their independent writing using the rubric.

Cool Tools: sticky notes (for compliments/suggestions), a toy microphone (a prop to use while reading one another's pieces aloud).

Guided Writing in Action

Guided writing is flexible. Here are some ways you can support your class with guided writing:

- Use guided writing immediately following modeled writing or shared writing to give students more practice before they write independently.

- Let the students write independently first, and discover what the students need to work on. The next day, try practicing those skills in guided writing cooperative groups.

- Skip the guided practice with the entire class if most of the students don't need it; pull together only the students who need the extra support.

In both classroom examples below, the modeled/shared writing step is followed by independent writing, which is then followed by guided writing. Sometimes teachers like to see what the students need to work on, then back up and offer guided practice the next day based on their observations. In either lesson the modeled/shared writing step could have been followed by group guided writing before the students were sent off to write on their own. Remember, there is no single "right" way to implement guided writing.

Scaffolded lesson

SECOND Graders Write Descriptions

"The jalapeno bread bagel feels smooth as a dish but it tastes as hot as fiery salsa," exclaims second grader Jaime as he tries a bite-sized piece of bagel. His class has just read *Jalepeño Bagels,* by Natasha Wing, and Mrs. Carpenter has decided to ask the students try some descriptive writing based on their senses and a hands-on tasting session. As part of her writing workshop, she is teaching the students to use interesting words and to compose written descriptions of an object in the classroom. The district assessment is around the corner, and she is also fitting in writing paragraphs with topic sentences. It feels like too much to include all these objectives in her lesson today, so she chooses to focus on sensory descriptions and word choice.

Identifying Examples

First the class reviews descriptions they have read in various books in the past week. Students read their examples aloud, and Mrs. Carpenter contributes some as well. They pay attention to how authors choose words, often including similes and metaphors to create word pictures in the mind of the reader.

Modeling/Shared Writing

Then Mrs. Carpenter leads the class in writing a shared description of jalapeno bagels based on each of the senses. She writes some of the sentences and invites the students to come up to help with others. When they are finished, the chart reads:

> The moist shiny bagel feels smooth as a dish when we run our fingers over its surface. It tastes as hot as fiery salsa burning our tongues. The smell of spicy jalapeno fills our noses. It tickles and makes our mouths water. Round as a dough-nut but tan like bread, the bagel calls for us to munch it down. So we take both hands and close our eyes. We tear off a moist bite and chomp away. Rip, rip, we tear and munch to get our fill for a snack. Chewy and fresh, the jalapeno bagel is as fresh as a spring morning. Close your eyes and enjoy!

Independent Writing

The students each take to their desks to write descriptions of any object in the class-room they choose. Mrs. Carpenter encourages them to talk with a partner before they start writing. She circulates through the room, and some students need help. Johnny admits he doesn't know what to write about: "There are too many choices." Mrs. Carpenter helps him select a quilt in the corner to describe. Sarah selects a new sponge by the sink and after running through all the senses says she doesn't know what to say about smell. Mrs. Carpenter asks her to reflect on what a sponge smells like after it has been used to wipe up a mess or been sprayed with a cleaning product.

As the class writing period rushes to a close, Mrs. Carpenter and I quickly assess the students' writing. We are pleased on the whole, but notice that many students have trouble varying their sentences and coming up with ideas to write about. We decide that tomorrow we will have them write descriptions together in guided writing groups. We hope this extra practice will help them add detail to their writing. I will also briefly model descriptive writing again, using a previous piece of shared writing.

Shared Writing (based on needs assessed in independent writing)

The next day I take over as guest teacher and lead a quick review of what makes a good description. The students tell me a description has to have adjectives or describing words that relate to the five senses. Next, I pull a banana out of my bag. The students brainstorm how they might describe it, using the five senses to trigger their reactions. I fill in a web on the overhead with their responses, adding details as we go:

> Sight—yellow, shaped like a crescent moon, fresh, like an old-fashioned telephone
>
> Touch—smooth like dolphin skin or a rubber ball
>
> Taste—sweet, squishy, tastes great dipped in chocolate
>
> Sound—ripping the skin off, soft munchy
>
> Smell—sweet

Together we write a shared description, carefully focusing on varied ways to start each sentence. In the beginning several students dictate sentences that start, "It is . . .." "It feels. . . ." I ask whether they notice anything, and hands go up as students report we have too many *it*s. To be funny and make a point I write *it* on a piece of paper and rip it up and march across the room to toss the paper into the trash can. I tell the class I'm going to try hard to not start any of the sentences with *it*, and I'll also try to use more interesting words to describe the banana. Our masterpiece of shared writing on the overhead looks like this:

> The little yellow banana is like a bright yellow moon shining at me from the bottom of my lunch box. As I grab the yummy fruit, the smooth skin feels like a rubber ball. When I munch on this treat, it squishes between my teeth. Sweet smells fill the air with banana mania!

We discuss alternate ways to begin descriptive sentences and come up with a list of them based on the senses:

> ### Ways to Describe Something/Sentence Starters
>
> Sight—The _____ is like a . . .
>   Try naming the object something other than itself.
>   *Example*—banana, juicy treat, healthy snack, yummy food
>
> Hearing—I love the way the . . .
>   Listen to . . .
>   Use noisy words
>   *Example*—munch, crunch, squirt
>
> Touch—When I touch _____ , it feels like a . . .
>   When my fingers meet the_____ , it feels . . .
>
> Taste—The _____ tastes like. . . .
>   The flavor of the _____ is just like . . .
>
> Smell—_____ fills the air.
>   Stop and enjoy the _____ smell.

Adapted from Mariconda 1999.

Guided Writing

On each table are several oranges, apples, or a bunch of grapes. Students, in groups, work on describing the fruit. Tasting makes this lesson a hit, especially since it's almost lunchtime. I assign each child to be "in charge of" a sense (touch, taste, sight, hearing, smell). The discussions are lively and joyful. I ask the children to take turns around their table giving a sentence describing the fruit in terms of their assigned sense.

Before passing out the sentence strips (strips of paper on which they will write their sentence descriptions), I model one for them. "Let's say I am in charge of describing what my banana looks like, then I might write, 'The little yellow crescent moon shines at me from the bottom of my lunch box.'"

As the students work, Mrs. Carpenter and I circulate, asking probing questions: "What do you say when you bite into a grape? How does it feel on your tongue? Is it noisy to eat?" We confer with each group and prompt individuals. At several

Figure 1.3

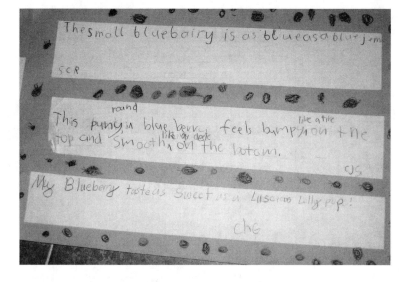

tables we notice the sentences start the same, with *the*, so we work together to change a couple of them. Some students are stuck, and we prompt them with questions. I tell Steven that the blueberry looks like a jewel. He ends up using a word he came up with, *gem*.

After a quick outdoor recess, each group negotiates an order for their strips. Even the most reluctant writers engage in this lively debate. I see strips moving around and students defending reasons for their order. (Some just want their own strip to be first in the poem; after all, they are only second graders!)

The end of the lesson draws to a close as I call each group up to stand in front of the empty overhead projector, our "spotlight" for the activity (Figure 1.3). Each group reads their description aloud, and the class gives them compliments. Here are some of our guided descriptions.

Mandarin Orange

The orange looks as small as a baseball.
When I drop it, it sounds like, thump!
Outside the mandarin is as squishy as a banana.
The mandarin tastes sweet and sour at the same time.
But the outside tastes <u>very, very</u> bad.
Do <u>not</u> eat the skin!
—Aren, Stephen, Humna, Claire

Apples

Apples taste wonderful like nothing you've ever tasted before.
The red ripe apple tastes delicious.
My apple tastes juicy like fresh fruit punch.
The red and yellow apple looks as round as a baseball.
Yum, it is good and tasty to eat in one bite.
This crunchy ripe snack made a "snap" sound

when the teacher cut it with the sharp kitchen knife.
Fresh apples smell like fruit punch.

—Rebecca, Jacob, Caiseen

Before dismissing the class for lunch, Mrs. Carpenter and I ask the students to reflect on and share with a partner what they learned about writing a description, and we add these ideas to the chart. The insights are revealing. Caiseen notes that sentences in a description shouldn't all start with "it" or "the." Others want to add that eating makes writing fun and so does working in a group. Tomorrow they'll be ready to try writing descriptions on their own again. The support of this added "middle piece" has provided the guidance and extra practice students needed (see Appendix C).

FOURTH Graders Respond to Literature

scaffolded lesson

"I think Mr. Washington is a kind neighbor and friend," explains fourth grader Jerome after the class has read *Sing to the Stars,* by Mary Brigid Barrett (1994). This picture book is the lovely story about the friendship between a boy, Ephram, and his elderly neighbor, Mr. Washington. In his prime, the older gentleman's nickname, Flash Fingers Washington, described his ability to play jazz, blues, and gospel on the piano. After a devastating car accident he loses his daughter, his sight, and his motivation to play the piano ever again. Ephram and Mr. Washington end up encouraging each other to play in a local community concert in the park. This simple yet touching story has moved me too, and I want to motivate the children to write about it.

Earlier I had decided that writing poetry would be an exciting way to respond to literature while fifty teachers are gathered around watching me teach. (The teachers are attending a yearlong district Title One course. Every time we meet, I demonstrate a lesson.) I chuckle to myself as I pull out my iPod and survey the large group forced to stand in a circle around the room (there's hardly room for them, let alone chairs). The teachers look like Dr. Seuss' Whos from Whosville after the Grinch has stolen Christmas.

The students, many of whom are English language learners, are spellbound by my iPod and they forget that they are surrounded by a mob of teachers. I set up the minispeakers and plug it in. They wait to see why I have brought such a cool artifact to their classroom. I ask them to review the main events in the story with a partner. Then we discuss the types of music presented in the story. I ask for volunteers to name all the kinds of music they can think of. Words pop up around the room: "Jazz." "Hip-hop." "Reggae," "Gospel." "Blues." "Rock and roll." "Country." I quickly run through the beginnings of various songs on the iPod and ask students to identify which type of music is being played. Their faces are filled with delight.

Identifying Examples

I use an overhead projector to display various "noisy poems" (see Chapter 3) that other students have written and ask the students to analyze and discuss what they like about the poems. Regie Routman's idea of sharing "kids' poems" as a motivation for writing works (Routman 2000). Students really pay attention. I save poetry from lessons at all grade levels and then select from five to seven student poems to open lessons on poetry writing. The students like the poems and have excellent comments: "They don't rhyme." "They have noisy words." "They use repetition."

Modeling

I tell the students that free verse would be an excellent way to express our thoughts, opinions, and feelings about the story. I carefully think aloud as I construct a poem about Mr. Washington on a projected transparency. ("I think I will use noisy words to add interest to my poem." "I think I can tell Mr. Washington's story through the poem while also talking about the kind person that he is.") The class watches while I struggle through my ideas, first on a web, then in a poem:

Mr. Washington

Flash Fingers Washington
Played it all in his day
Bam, boom, bing
Now he listens to
The music of footsteps
In the dark
Tap, tap, tap
Caring and kind
He shares the music
Of his soul
Flash Fingers Washington

We reread the poem, and the students tell me they like the noisy words, or onomatopoeia, and the repetition of the first and last line.

Shared Writing

Based on the students' contributions during the identifying and modeling steps of the lesson, I sense that this group isn't quite ready to write. So I ask for a volunteer to come up to the overhead to write a poem with me in front of the class. Josie willingly offers to try. I decide not to put her on the spot in front of everyone. She dictates and I write for her on a projected transparency. At various points we ask other students to contribute ideas and lines. Here's the completed poem:

Ephram
by Josie

The strings of the violin
Mr. Washington's handshake
Tap, tap, tap, boom
Stage fright filled his soul

> Tap, tap, tap, boom
> His music filled the air
> with sweet music.

The class rereads the poem and compliments Josie's efforts. This writer beams with pride!

Independent Writing

The lesson provided students with lots of support: the student samples, my modeling, and Josie's modeling. So instead of asking groups of students to work on poems, I ask the students to write poems on their own. I want to see what they can do. (Tomorrow we can write guided poems in groups if we need to.) Many of the students dive in and scribble poems down like crazy. I move around to the ones who just sit and stare, asking questions and offering assistance. At the end of the period I collect the literature response poems. Overall I am pleased. The observing teachers, whom I have tried to forget as I've worked with the children, are impressed at the ease with which students produced quality writing in a very short time. Frankly, so am I! Here are some examples:

Ephram

by Kathleen

The night dances across
The piano
Stars twinkle, twinkle, twinkle

Ephram

by Sierrah

Ephram plays beautiful classical violin music
Mmm, ding, mmmmdong
But stage fright filled him.
His music sings to the stars
The stars dance around to the melody.

Ephram

by Michael

Sees the notes flowing in the air
Hears the music
Touches the string with a sweet rhythm
And feels his soul dancing
Boom, tap, boom, tap

Guided Writing

In the next lesson, the students read their poems in front of the class. Then they list what they like, and we form a rudimentary sort of rubric. These guidelines include repeating lines or words, incorporating noisy words, using similes or metaphors, and including feelings. At this point, after they have struggled through their own poems,

I often offer support by way of guided groups. I ask groups of students to choose a character from another book the class has read and, using the rubric as a guide, to write a poem about this character. I circulate among the groups as they write, offering assistance and probing for more ideas and language.

An Ending Celebration

One of the best parts of this lesson takes place at the very end. In the story, the boy, Ephram, and the elderly blind gentleman, Mr. Washington, play the song "Amazing Grace" under the stars at the community concert in the park. When I ask whether students know the song, I discover that almost half of them have never heard the gospel tune before. I figure that with fifty teachers in the room, certainly someone can easily belt it out for us. I am right. I ask for a volunteer, and one talented teacher steps up and sings a quiet, spine-tingly a cappella version of the first verse. Silence and admiration hang in the air and unite us all, teachers and students alike. Then the group slowly breaks into a round of appreciative applause. Wouldn't it be great if our students clapped after all our lessons? The magical power of music, free verse, and guided writing made the lesson a success!

Discussion Questions

1. What did you already know about guided writing before reading the chapter? Have your ideas changed? How? What questions do you have about it now?

2. Construct a KWL chart for yourself or your study group:
    What I/We Know About Guided Writing /
    What I/We Want to Know/What I / We Learned

3. Why isn't modeling enough sometimes? Give an example of a time you modeled and students had difficulty moving into independent writing. How might guided writing help?

4. What is guided writing? How do literacy experts define it? After trying guided writing in your classroom, identify three key words you'd use to define it.

5. Review the settings for guided writing lessons and consider which ones might work best for your students. Which appeals most to you and why?

6. List the steps of a scaffolded writing lesson that you already use in your lessons. Which steps are new to you? Which steps do you think are not necessary every time? Why?

Try It in Your Classroom

- Choose one of the sample lessons/examples in this chapter (describing a story setting, describing a piece of fruit, or responding to literature with poetry) and try it with your class. Discuss with your colleagues what went well and your questions/concerns about teaching guided writing.

✐ Choose one of the settings for guided writing (whole-class table groups, temporary groups during writing workshop based on need, a weeklong temporary intervention group) and try it with your students.

Chapter Two

Using Scaffolded Writing Steps, Cool Tools, and Graphic Organizers

I like to write. It lets my imagination fly.
—Malik

"That was really fun, Mrs. O." "When can we do that again?" "Yeah, I wish it wasn't over yet!" "When are you coming back?" These are the magic words I want to hear from students after I teach a guided writing lesson (or any writing lesson for that matter).

Guided writing is not only an effective teaching option for improving student writing but also an enjoyable experience for students and teachers alike. What makes it fun is that students feel successful as they work in guided teams with cool tools. When we scaffold instruction for our budding writers, they understand and enjoy writing more. To help you understand guided writing within the context of a scaffolded lesson, this chapter provides an explanation of each step, some quick examples from a variety of grade levels, and ideas for keeping students actively engaged and interested.

Cool tools (a kid-friendly term) and graphic organizers are concrete ways of keeping students on track during writing and giving them additional support throughout the writing process. You can pick and choose from the ideas here and adapt them to any writing skill or genre you are teaching at your grade level.

Concrete Supports for Guided Writing

There are many creative ways to use graphic organizers during guided writing lessons. Keep in mind that graphic organizers are an *option,* not a requirement. Some common graphic organizers are pictured in Figure 2.1. Sentence patterns lifted from books may also provide the fill-in support some writers need to organize their own voice and ideas. Outlines offer support for challenging skills like writing paragraphs, narratives, or reports. The key is to use them as long as the support is necessary and then wean students away from them so that the organization doesn't become stilted. Many of the struggling writers and second language learners I work with respond particularly well to graphic organizers, both as we write together and as they begin to write on their own.

As they brainstorm, students may fill in graphic organizers with ideas for writing as well as possible details. Using circular "weekend webs" (see Chapter 4), students can brainstorm what they did over the weekend, adding details that flow out from the main ideas. From these possibilities, they are able to select one idea and

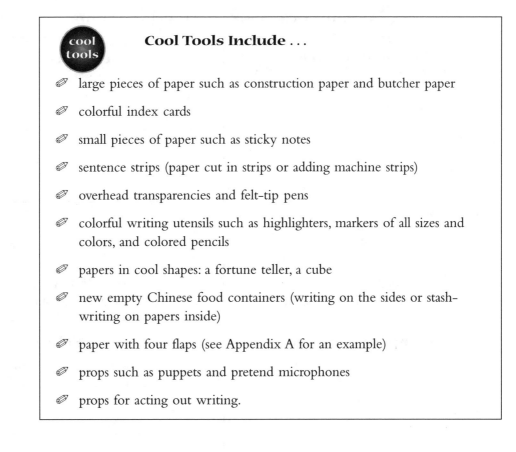

Cool Tools Include . . .

cool tools

- large pieces of paper such as construction paper and butcher paper
- colorful index cards
- small pieces of paper such as sticky notes
- sentence strips (paper cut in strips or adding machine strips)
- overhead transparencies and felt-tip pens
- colorful writing utensils such as highlighters, markers of all sizes and colors, and colored pencils
- papers in cool shapes: a fortune teller, a cube
- new empty Chinese food containers (writing on the sides or stash-writing on papers inside)
- paper with four flaps (see Appendix A for an example)
- props such as puppets and pretend microphones
- props for acting out writing.

zero in on that part of the organizer, adding more spokes and ideas as needed. (Second grader Griffin's weekend web and the paragraph he wrote based on it are shown in Figure 2.2.)

A patterned writing form has blanks for students to fill in to emulate the writing style and organization of a particular book or story. For example, a class of fourth graders had read *My Mama Had a Dancing Heart* (1995), by Libba Gray (see Chapter 5). I had them loosely follow the pattern of the book and begin and end their pieces by adapting Gray's line, "My mama had a dancing heart and she shared that heart with me." The students observed me write using the pattern, participated in small-group guided writing, and finally filled in their own ideas. Some students wrote about dogs or cats with playful hearts, while others plugged special family members into the pattern.

Patterned text can be used with students of all ages as a way to teach voice and organization (see Chapter 5). However, if we overrely on patterned text, our students' writing may become too formulaic. I have worked in some primary classrooms in which innovations on published stories dominate the writing program. These students don't progress nearly as well as those in classrooms where patterned text is just one in a balanced mix of supports. Therefore, while I enjoy using patterns, I do so sparingly and instead encourage students to venture into their own creative style.

A more elaborate graphic organizer is a form students fill out while writing a particular genre (a narrative or report, for example). The form might have boxes

Figure 2.1

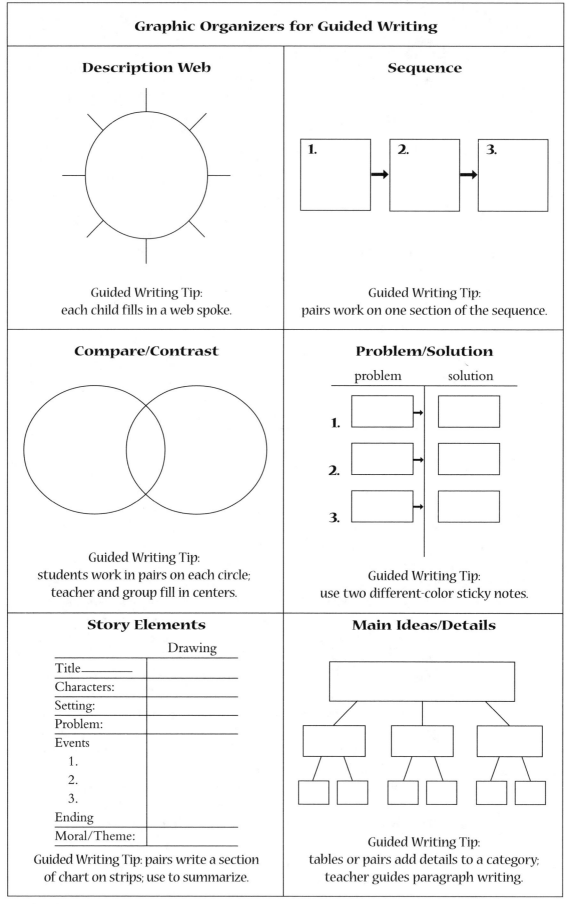

Graphic Organizers for Guided Writing

Description Web

Guided Writing Tip:
each child fills in a web spoke.

Sequence

1.
2.
3.

Guided Writing Tip:
pairs work on one section of the sequence.

Compare/Contrast

Guided Writing Tip:
students work in pairs on each circle;
teacher and group fill in centers.

Problem/Solution

problem   solution

1.
2.
3.

Guided Writing Tip:
use two different-color sticky notes.

Story Elements

Drawing

Title_____
Characters:
Setting:
Problem:
Events
   1.
   2.
   3.
Ending
Moral/Theme:

Guided Writing Tip: pairs write a section
of chart on strips; use to summarize.

Main Ideas/Details

Guided Writing Tip:
tables or pairs add details to a category;
teacher guides paragraph writing.

Figure 2.2

Griffin's Organizer

BBQ (center of organizer, with branches to: hot flare, jusy chicken, marinat chiken, rice, milk)

(Title) BBQ

Wow" flanes were flying up and smoking into the night sky as the juicy chicken got on the grill. Before we BBQ we hedged weed-wacked and we mowed the back lawn. After we took off the chicken and made some rice a ronie, and mash patato. We poured a ice cold glass of milk and ate all our dinner.

for portions of the writing, blanks to fill in, and sometimes even sentence starters. Here are some examples:

> When I teach students to write stories, we first read stories, then I write a story in front of them using a form for each element. For example, when I write the story beginning, I use a form that includes a checklist of choices: a "noisy" word, or onomatopoeia; a quote; a description; or an action. The students then write the beginning of their own story using the same form. As I continue to model describing the setting, characters, problem, resolution, and ending, I use a similar form for each element. The students then practice writing stories—in guided groups and alone—using these forms. I wean them away from the forms after they have written a few stories and internalized the process.

✐ Many teachers use a pattern form like the one in Figure 2.3 for teaching students to write paragraphs or even five-paragraph essays.

✐ When I introduce elementary students to report writing, I project a transparency of the graphic organizer in Figure 2.4 as I write the opening paragraph. Then I circulate among the guided writing groups and help them as they work their way through the model using their own copies of the form. Finally, students write independently using the same organizer. After using the form a few times we put it away, but continue to check whether our opening paragraphs contain the necessary ingredients. Below is an example of a group of fifth graders' opening report paragraph. Their teacher, Mrs. Musante, conferred with each guided writing group over the course of a week. Each student was "in charge" of a sentence strip containing one of the parts of an opening paragraph. As a team, the group assembled and checked their sentences and then combined them into a paragraph.

Hurricane: Storm of Disaster

by Table 3

Interesting Beginning: A swirling mass of wind comes hurtling through the air, destroying everything in its path.

Thesis Statement: Without a doubt hurricanes are one of the Earth's strongest natural weather disasters.

Topic Sentence and sneak preview of three main points of the paper: Hurricanes are mostly wind and you will learn in the following paragraphs how hurricanes are made. You will also learn that it's hard to predict when hurricanes are formed, where they're going to hit, but there are some tools that help people predict them.

✐ When teaching students to write a compare/contrast essay, Eddie Garcia and Tina Randolph, teachers in a Southern California middle school in which many students are English language learners, first model in front of the class on a form; class members follow along, stay engaged, and contribute as they fill in their copies of the same form. Then Eddie and Tina meet with small groups who write on another topic using the forms. Finally, students use the forms again when they write independently. (Eddie and Tina use graphic organizers for every genre they teach.) Guided writing with graphic organizers has helped these teachers dramatically improve student writing.

Scaffolded lesson

SCAFFOLDED Writing Steps and the Role of Guided Writing: A Closer Look

Guided writing instruction will benefit your students most if the lessons are interesting to learn and fun to teach. The following detailed explanations of each step of a scaffolded writing lesson incorporate creative ways to engage students using cool tools that become informal assessments.

Figure 2.3

Paragraph Graphic Organizer

Topic Sentence: _____

_____

_____

_____

Supporting Detail 1: _____

_____

_____

_____

Supporting Detail 2: _____

_____

_____

_____

Supporting Detail 3: _____

_____

_____

_____

Restate topic sentence: _____

_____

_____

_____

Figure 2.4

Opening Report Paragraph Organizer

Interesting Beginning (fact, quote, descriptions, question, dialogue, opinion, problem):

_____

_____

_____

_____

_____

_____

Thesis Statement:

_____

_____

_____

_____

_____

_____

Topic Sentence (includes preview of three main points of the paper):

_____

_____

_____

_____

_____

Although the most effective way to teach something new is usually to follow the sequence in order, the scaffolding model is flexible. Once you have helped students identify the skill, strategy, or genre in other authors' writing, modeled the writing for them, and led them in shared writing, whether and to what extent you use guided writing depends on your writers' needs. You decide how much support they need before they write on their own. And after they've written independently, you may want to go back and reinforce the learning using any of the preceding steps. What I love about scaffolding is the many interesting options it provides for helping students learn to write.

Before we begin our in-depth look at the process, let me define the steps once again and pose a question or two to think about in relation to them:

- *Identifying examples*: Show examples of the writing skill, strategy, or genre you are teaching in literature, books, magazines, or other texts. You may also use student samples. *Can my students identify in literature and texts the aspect of writing I am teaching?*

- *Modeling*: Model the writing skill, strategy, or genre by writing in front of your students. Don't just explain what you would write, actually write and think aloud while doing so. *As my students watch me write, can they turn to a partner and comment on what they are learning as I write? Can they give a thumbs-up or thumbs-down or write a response on a slate?*

- *Shared writing*: Write together. Let the students dictate while you help them compose and serves as a scribe. *How do my students participate as we write together? What do their contributions reveal? Can they write an individual contribution on a slate?*

- *Guided writing*: Either have students work in teams at tables as you spend a few minutes with each one, or form a specific-needs group to work with more extensively. Either students each take a portion of the topic to write on and combine their efforts, or they write independently and then discuss the results under your guidance. *How do my students write when held responsible for a portion of the writing? What is working and what do they need help with? Do they understand the skill, strategy, or genre? How are they doing when they write portions of their own pieces during the guided writing group?*

- *Independent writing*: Ask students to write on their own. *Can my students apply what we have modeled, shared, and learned in guided practice? Are they getting the concept, or do I need to back up and identify more examples, model more writing, or introduce more shared or guided practice?*

- *Guided conferring*: Confer with small groups and individuals using the rubric you have developed together as a guide. In group shares, be sure students give one another compliments, ask questions, and make suggestions. *What do the students understand? What do they need help with?*

Identifying Examples

When we use published texts as models, students do some of their best writing. We need to take advantage of this fact and ask students to read like writers and notice what authors do. The purpose of this step is for students to search for examples of the particular genre, strategy, or writing skill in books, magazines, even exemplary student work. You can ask, "How do authors and writers use this skill [strategy, genre] in their work? How does it help them? How can it help us when we write too?"

You can introduce the lesson in one of two ways (both are effective, so you can vary your approach):

🖉 Tell students the genre, skill, or strategy you are going to teach and how it helps them write. Then show them examples. Suggested language: *Today we will learn how various authors begin nonfiction texts so that you can use the same types of beginnings in your reports and other nonfiction writing.* Or: *We are going to learn about [genre, skill, strategy], which will help you with your writing by [describe]. Let's see how authors do this in their writing.*

🖉 Have the students state the genre, skill, or strategy and tell how it will help them write after looking at examples. Suggested language: *Class, today we are going to learn about an important technique writers use in their work. As we look at each example, think about these questions: What is this author doing? What do you notice? How does this help the writing? What can we call this writing technique? How can you use this in your writing?* Sometimes I use Katie Wood Ray's chart (see Figure 2.5) as a graphic organizer. Staff developer and author Janet Angelillo (2002) even uses this chart when students hunt for examples of punctuation in their reading.

After students have searched your classroom library and the school library for examples of a particular writing genre or strategy (beginning, ending, paragraph, description, report, thesis, etc.), you can begin a rubric, or list of criteria. You'll add to this rubric throughout the lesson as the students gain more insights and experience with the writing element they are studying. Don't worry if they don't have a complete picture immediately. After a few more steps and more exposure to the skill or genre, they will have more to say.

The examples encountered during this step can become points of reference all year long. For example, one class of third graders I worked with on developing plot and suspense (Mariconda 1999) used an example we found in an adapted version of *Tom Sawyer*. The students analyzed the way the author built suspense through Becky's and Tom's emotional reactions to a series of noises when they were hiding in the cave. We referred to this example often as the students developed problems and scenes in their own stories.

Cool Tools for Identifying Examples

I like to copy a page or two from a text we've read that students can mark with colored pencils and highlighters. (Highlighter tape works well on originals that you don't want to ruin.) For example, when studying paragraphs, a class of fifth graders took paragraphs in their *Explorer National Geographic* magazines and highlighted the topic sentence in one color, the thesis statement in another color, and the supporting details in still another color. Another class of sixth graders marked examples of beginnings from nonfiction books with sticky notes. They then read them aloud

Figure 2.5

Identifying an Author's Craft, Techniques, and Skills

What is the author doing? (describe techniques, examples)	Why is the author doing this?	What can I name this technique?	What are examples from other books?	How can I use this in my writing?
Technique #1				
Technique #2				
Technique #3				

©1999 by Katie Wood Ray, from from *Wondrous Words* (NCTE: Urbana, IL). Used with permission.

Tips for Charting Author's Craft, Techniques, and Skills

Hunt through books and find examples of craft, techniques, and writing skills to plug into this chart. Here are some of the skills and techniques you might have students search for and then analyze. Make sure they rename the techniques and tell *how* the technique or skill helps the writing.

✐ *Hunt for Author's Craft/Techniques, including:*
- overall organization of text—Is it a problem, solution, memoir, descriptive, personal narrative, circular, see-saw text?
- descriptive language
- plot development
- use of metaphors
- development of suspense
- sequence of events
- organization of nonfiction text such as question and answer, cause and effect, sequence of events, and compare/contrast
- nonfiction text features
- use of dialogue
- repetition of events, language
- ways to show emotions of characters

✐ *Hunt for Skills*
- sentence fluency
- use of punctuation in dialogue
- commas and other conventions
- paragraphing, topic sentences, opening and closing sentences

and came up with names for the types of beginnings. Acting can also be a cool tool. A class of first graders acted out the beginnings of a number of stories.

Identifying Examples in Action

During a unit on descriptive writing, Mrs. Carpenter's second graders read *Cloudy with a Chance of Meatballs* (1978), by Judi Barrett. They identified descriptive language in the book and visualized, drew, and acted out several sections. To give the students further practice in identifying descriptive language, Mrs. Carpenter shared a former student's personal narrative about losing a tooth in a piece of chocolate cake at a restaurant. Each pair of students were given a copy of the story and used crayons to underline the sensory descriptions. The student sample provided additional exposure to the type of language the students were expected to produce. They were spellbound, because they knew the author, now a big fourth grader!

Modeling

Teacher modeling is critical, yet often we're in such a hurry to get to the assignment and the kids' own writing that we're tempted to skip it. We must also be careful to *really model* rather than just explain the assignment. Here's an example:

Mrs. Ramos' third graders are learning how to write a friendly letter and have been reading various trade books that contain letters, including *Dear Daddy* (1985), by Phillippe Dupasquier, and *Dear Mr. Blueberry* (1991), by Simon James. Mrs. Ramos asks pairs and table groups to discuss what they noticed about the letters in these books and records the students' pointers on a chart titled "Tips for Writing Friendly Letters."

Modeling Scenario 1 (the ideal: Write in front of students.)

On a projected transparency, Mrs. Ramos writes a friendly letter to her cousin in Colorado, thinking aloud as she composes. *Boys and girls, I can't remember where to put the date. Oh, yeah, I could look at the pointers and that will help me.* She continues in this vein, stopping to ponder which word to use, what to say next, and the spellings of various words. After she finishes writing three paragraphs in front of the students, she closes the letter with a few questions for her cousin and the salutation. Mrs. Ramos asks the students to tell her what they noticed about how she wrote the letter and adds their comments to the class chart.

Modeling Scenario 2 (Explaining is *not* modeling.)

Mrs. Ramos holds up a blank piece of paper and points to a copy of one of the example letters that has been posted on the bulletin board. *This is how you will write your letter. Let's say I wanted to write a letter to my cousin. I'd put the date here* [points], *and salutation there* [points], *and in each new paragraph I'd tell her about what each of my kids is doing. Then I'd ask her a few questions. Then I'd sign off here and write my name.* She passes out paper and students begin to write.

In the second, shortcut, version, Mrs. Ramos does give an example, but she doesn't take the time to get into the nitty-gritty and write a letter sentence by sentence, word by word, in front of the children. She *explains* the assignment, rather than *models* it. While modeling takes a bit longer, the payoffs are enormous. Students learn more and write better when they see a model and get a feel for the process.

What If You're Afraid to Write in Front of Students?

Modeling writing may be more comfortable for you if you compose the piece ahead of time and then later pretend you are writing it for the first time. This way, you'll have thought through your teaching points ahead of time. I don't do this very often. I prefer the natural struggle of writing in front of the students for the first time. However, on my way to school, I may toss around a topic in my mind and think of some things I might say. Whatever approach you take, be sure to ask questions like these aloud to make your think-aloud authentic:

- *What should I say next?*

- *Let me think about what word to put here.*

- *I am stuck on spelling a word.*

- *I think I will change that part. It doesn't sound right.*

- *I left something out here.*

Teachers tell me all the time, "Oh, modeling writing is easy for you. You're a writer." Although writing does come naturally to me, I am a horrific speller. Sometimes, for the life of me, I can't remember how to spell even the most common words. To make matters worse, when I conduct demonstration lessons, many teachers are watching. I begin with the disclaimer that although I am a poor speller, I always choose the most interesting word whether I can spell it or not. I circle words I can't spell in my think-aloud and explain the benefit of just going on and correcting them later. So in a way, my spelling deficit works in my favor. Students appreciate this advice and don't feel so alone in their spelling struggles.

cool tools
Cool Tools for Modeling

We're the ones using the tools here, like writing on a transparency or funky-shaped paper. However, sometimes I do have students come up to my draft and underline parts of it or attach a sticky note with an insight or a compliment.

Drama is a favorite cool tool of mine. When I am writing my draft, I often stop and ask students to act out part of what I am writing to see if it makes sense. For example, when I modeled my shark story for a class of first graders, I had the kids pretend to be me talking to the instructor, shaking nervously, jumping in the water and holding my breath, and looking around at the underwater world. Having students act out the events helps you model and gives you ideas for what comes next. I also ask students to give me a thumbs-up or a thumbs-down when they agree or disagree with something I am adding to my draft.

After you model, you can ask students to turn to partners and tell what they liked and noticed about your writing (Routman 2000). Then it is helpful to return to the rubric or list you are compiling with the class and add their insights.

Sometimes during my guided writing lessons I also model for the small group or individual student. Doing so orally is often enough, but many times I'll quickly write another example they can see.

Shared Writing

Student engagement increases during shared writing, because you and your students are writing together. You'll usually be doing the writing while guiding the students' discussion about what to record. Shared writing is fun, easy, and a great way for students to learn how to write whatever you're teaching. I usually write on a projected transparency in upper grades and on chart paper in lower grades. Either way, I save the work so we can refer to it in other lessons and perhaps add to it over time. (Sometimes it becomes an ongoing saga spread over several days or longer.)

There is a misconception that shared writing is just for little kids. That isn't true. Primary teachers do use the technique in their morning messages and group-composed chart stories. However, older students enjoy shared writing too. It gives them one more demonstration and some practice before they have to write on their own, and they appreciate the extra support.

During a shared writing lesson the group discusses the topic, negotiates each word and sentence, and rereads constantly to clarify the piece and decide what should come next. Shared writing works for any skill or genre you want to teach: persuasive writing, descriptive writing—you name it.

Asking a Student to Model

A creative way to vary shared writing is to call up just one student to write in front of the class. I assist just as I do when the whole class is writing together, asking probing questions about topic order and details. The student writer thinks aloud, and we discuss word choice and ideas, often calling on other students to help. I find the class really pays attention: watching a peer up front grabs them. You can hear a pin drop. Of course, everyone compliments the guest writer before he or she sits back down.

Sometimes you'll want to write for the volunteer student as he or she dictates. This is an especially appropriate strategy with kindergartners, first graders, second language learners, and reluctant writers.

Cool Tools for Shared Writing

Students are usually engaged and involved during a shared writing lesson. I like to have them give thumbs-up or thumbs-down signals for word choice, and so forth. Also, the students can write interesting words or ideas on slates or in the air. Sticky notes are another way of ensuring that students keep their brains going during the shared writing lesson.

After a shared writing lesson, you can ask students to think about what they have learned and share their insights with their partner or tablemates. Then they can share these insights with the class as you add them to the chart or rubric you are building together.

Sometimes when I meet with a guided writing group that is working on a piece together and the energy is flagging, I take over the pen for a moment and become the coach and scribe. This instance of shared writing is just what they need to spur them on.

Guided Writing

Guided writing is the magic "middle piece," a way to give students more support but also more responsibility before they write on their own. The goal is for a small group of students to write together, with every member participating. You may circulate from group to group or work with a single group with similar needs. The students either write the piece together, each student contributing a portion, or write independently and then share what they have written with you and the other group members and develop the piece based on the feedback they receive. Either way, the students use the rubric they've helped construct during the other parts of the lesson to guide them and are supported by your vigilant coaching. Guided writing may take place either immediately after modeled or shared writing (to provide more practice before writing independently) or after independent writing (when you have observed students as they write and looked at the writing they've produced and decided what they need to work on).

There are four ways to use guided writing:

1. during whole-class lessons

2. in small guided writing or guided reading groups

3. as an intervention

4. during writing workshop.

You choose when and for how long you wish to incorporate any of these options. Figures 2.6 through 2.9 summarize the details of these options.

Independent Writing

This is the critical "quiet time" when all pencils hit the paper (you hope). After you have motivated your students with examples, models, and group writing experiences, it is their turn to experiment and write. Your earlier scaffolds have prepared students for this moment. Just how many steps you take them through before encouraging them to write on their own depends on your students and the difficulty of the writing task. Sometimes you may feel they are ready to experiment with writing alone right after you have modeled the genre or strategy. Other times you may offer tons more support via shared and guided writing before turning them loose on their own. At some point, though, what students need is time to write independently every day!

If you notice certain students struggling over their writing and not making progress, you might meet with each of them individually or call them together as a group for some quick guided practice—or even additional modeling.

Figure 2.6

Guided Writing During Whole-Class Lessons

Use Modeled or Shared Writing

✏ First conduct a class lesson featuring modeled or shared writing.

✏ Once you have a list of guidelines for the assignment, you can meet with cooperative groups or convene a group to work with you.

Meet with Cooperative Table Groups

Use cool tools for a group composition.

✏ Each student contributes to a composition the group will share with the class.

✏ Students work as a team. A scribe writes on butcher paper, construction paper, or a transparency, or each student records a portion of the writing on a sentence strip, a piece of adding machine tape, or a sticky note, and the group glues the sections down in an order that makes sense.

Rotate among groups to confer/guide.

✏ Ask probing questions and have the students read their writing aloud. Support individuals who are not participating or seem stuck.

✏ Read strong examples aloud to the entire class: *Class, listen to this.*

✏ Ask the entire class for help: *This group is having trouble with such-and-so. Maybe your group is too. What can we do?*

Share/add to rubric.

✏ Ask each group to come up to the front and read their piece. (They might be "spotlighted" by the overhead projector, use a pretend microphone, act out their writing, or make a quick drawing on a projected transparency.)

✏ Lead the class in summarizing what they learned from writing in groups.

✏ Add these insights to a class rubric.

Assemble Groups Based on Needs

Study writing behavior and samples.

✏ Look over your students' writing samples to determine what they need to work on.

✏ Create one or more groups with similar needs. They might need practice in a genre, conventions (terminal punctuation, capitalization), or a specific writing strategy (adding sensory details, creating an interesting beginning).

Lead the guided writing session.

✏ Meet with these groups, one at a time, while the rest of the class is writing or reading. Either each student will contribute to a group piece, or the group will share and discuss pieces they have written independently.

✏ Work with the group for ten or fifteen minutes. Guide their responses.

✏ Discuss or model needs/problems. For example, if they are all stuck on brainstorming, model brainstorming ways you might develop a topic of your own and then have them brainstorm for a few minutes on their own piece.

✏ Use cool tools like sticky notes or special markers to make the session special and fun.

✏ Ask them to summarize their learning.

✏ Send the students back to their desks to write independently.

✏ Call the group together again if necessary.

Figure 2.7

Guided Writing in Small Groups

Consider Your Options

- Remember that guided writing isn't necessarily parallel to guided reading, so you don't have to set up formal needs-based writing groups that you meet with each week. (You may of course use that model if it fits your teaching style, grade level, and schedule, but no teacher should feel obligated to assign all students to small writing groups all the time!)
- You can occasionally use guided writing during guided reading.
- You could set up temporary, small, guided writing groups to introduce a genre like poetry or report writing.
- You could meet with a different group each day, or form temporary groups with students who need help or a challenge with a special project.

Meet During Guided Reading

Read a text together and write a response.

- Analyze the text.
- Model writing a summary or other kind of response (perhaps an innovation on the pattern or writing style).
- Choose cool tools like sentence strips, butcher paper, or sticky notes on which students each write a portion of a group response. Confer with students as they write.
- Together, add transitions and combine the individual contributions into a group piece.
- Prompt each student to write her or his own piece, as you and the other students in the group offering constant support. Some of the writing may be completed during whole-class lessons or writing workshop.

Meet with Guided Writing Groups

Study student writing and form one or more groups based on need.

- Look over your students' writing after you have introduced a new skill, and group students with similar needs.
- Circulate among the groups.
- You might work exclusively with one group for a week or so until their piece is done, then disband the group.

Use cool tools.

- Use cool tools like different colors and sizes of papers, sticky notes, and sentence strips.
- Try using overhead transparencies. Students love them.
- You might have upper-grade students lay out their pieces using a typesetting computer program or prepare a PowerPoint™ presentation.

Add to a rubric.

- Throughout the lesson have students help you add to a rubric or a "how to write a . . ." list.
- Elicit their insights after writing together.
- Ask them first to turn to a partner and tell what they learned about the aspect of writing they are studying and then share as a group.

Figure 2.8

Guided Writing as an Intervention

Form a Group

- Identify the neediest writers in your room and pull them into a group. They may include some of your special-needs students or English language learners.

Meet with the Group Regularly

- Provide writing instruction several times a week.

OR

Meet with the Group Occasionally

- Meet when a new writing genre or particularly difficult skill is introduced.
- Meet when the class is learning to write descriptions or reports.

Add More Knowledgeable Peers to the Group

- Put a student or two in the group who are already proficient in the skill or strategy so students will benefit from working with a more knowledgeable peer.

Cool Tools Rule!

- Cool tools are especially important in making writing fun and more concrete for students who struggle.
- Expecting them to write short contributions will enable struggling writers to feel successful and supported.
- The use of real objects (or photographs of drawings of real objects) will also help you scaffold the lessons.

Back Up and Reuse Modeled and Shared Writing

- These students need more demonstrations before they can practice effectively. Model writing in the group.
- Compose a shared piece while you serve as scribe.
- Return to these steps any time students need more support.

Use and Add to the Class Rubric

- Refer often to the class rubric.
- Help them understand what it means.
- Allow students to add to the rubric.

The rubric you have created during the other portions of the scaffolded lesson becomes the gold standard that guides students as they write. You might even leave the modeled, shared, and guided writing samples out for students to refer to.

Guided Conferring

Does this sound familiar? The line of students waiting to confer with you starts at your desk and snakes around the room. Conferring with individuals is an ef-

Figure 2.9

Guided Writing During Writing Workshop

Writing Workshop Basics

✐   Writing workshop may be held once or twice a week or every day, depending on the grade level and classroom, and includes these elements:

   ✐   **Teacher minilesson** (10 to 15 minutes).

   ✐   **Writing time** (20 to 30 minutes); students write on topics of their choice (or occasionally to a prompt) while you confer with individuals or small groups; students also confer with their peers.

   ✐   **Sharing time** (5 to 10 minutes); students take turns sitting in the author's chair reading their writing aloud. Other students offer compliments and questions.

   You can use small-group guided writing during any of these segments when you want to reinforce a difficult skill or new genre. Students gain new skills to incorporate into their own writing when writing workshop continues on subsequent days.

Emphasize a Teaching Point Made During the Minilesson

✐   Give students a rubric to guide them as they write their group piece based on the strategy or genre you've modeled.

✐   Rotate from table to table offering help and guidance.

✐   Add to the class rubric for the strategy or genre.

Use Guided Writing During Writing Time

✐   Pull together a small group to make a teaching point, either guiding their individual writing or composing a quick group piece. (For example, a group writes a paragraph together, then the students apply what they just learned to their own writing.)

Share Guided Writing Group Projects

✐   Have guided writing groups share their writing at the end of the workshop and invite their peers to respond.

---

fective way to teach and reinforce writing skills, but it can be such a frustrating logistical nightmare. In a guided conference a small group of students (between four and eight) reflect on their writing under your careful leadership (see Figure 2.10). This type of conference doesn't replace individual conferences, but it is a great alternative for reaching more students when you can't get to each one. Also, conferring with you in a small group like this teaches students how to confer with one another.

Here are some helpful hints for conducting guided conferences:

✐   *Begin with quick partner comments.* Ask students to read their work to a partner in the group, and have the partner give a compliment and ask a question. Then ask the partners to share these thoughts with the group.

✐   *Focus the conference on the task at hand.* Ask, "What are you having trouble writing? What is the hard part?" Bring the class-created rubric for the work

Figure 2.10

at hand. Ask each pair or individual writer to look for the items on the list one at a time. Use cool tools to help them remember what they've learned.

✐ *Let your students hold the pen.* Nobody likes red marks all over their writing! Besides, they probably won't internalize anything if you take over. Let the *students* wield the "magic" correction pen or attach the sticky note, not you. (Thanks to teachers Carol Levin and Kirstin Choy!) They will pay better attention, and this method of revising and editing is more respectful of the writer.

✐ *Back up to previous scaffolding steps if necessary.* If students need more modeling or practice, try returning to modeled or shared writing.

✐ *Have the students reflect on what they've learned.* Before the group disbands, ask the students to turn to a partner and verbalize what they learned in the session. Then ask one or two students to share their insights with everyone.

Discussion Questions

1. What are cool tools and how can they help you engage students in writing lessons? How can you use cool tools to assess your next steps? How will you know students are getting the point of the lesson? If you've tried incorporating cool tools into your writing lessons, what did you notice about student engagement?

2. How do your students respond when you use a variety of examples (to include published books and other students' work) of a genre or strategy?

3. Discuss Katie Wood Ray's chart in Figure 2.5. Give an example of a strategy or skill you need to teach this week and talk about how you will use the chart. After using the chart, reflect on how the lesson went. Which step of the chart is most helpful to students at your grade level? Which is the most difficult for your students to discuss?

4. Describe the difference between modeling and simply explaining, and give examples. Think back on an assignment that you explained rather than modeled. What happened? Why is modeling more effective?

5. Talk about how to use a class-created rubric during the modeled and shared writing portions of a lesson. Where would you display the rubric? How might you make it more accessible to students to use in groups and at their desks during independent writing?

Try It in Your Classroom

- Choose one of the guided writing models from this chapter that you haven't yet used and try it out. Share and discuss student samples with your colleagues.

- Experiment with some of the cool tools in this chapter. Which ones did your class like the best? Why? Explain how you use a cool tool as an informal assessment to guide your instruction.

- Use a graphic organizer or framing device during a guided writing lesson. How did the students respond? What worked? What more do you need to do to support students in their writing?

- Teach a fully scaffolded set of lessons: identifying examples, modeling, shared writing, guided writing, and independent writing. Reflect on how the students respond. Share your observations, student samples, and questions with your colleagues.

Chapter Three

Finding Your Voice: Noisy Poems

When I write poetry I think of what's important. It's like painting a picture and it doesn't even have to rhyme!
—Callie

What do you think of when you hear the word *poetry*? A coffeehouse where beatniks beat bongo drums while cool cats recite the lyrics of their latest hip creations? Robin Williams as a teacher in the thought-provoking movie *Dead Poets Society* urging his high school students to dive deeply into the works of famous poets? Do you cringe because somebody, somewhere, sometime made you read and write poetry that you just didn't care about? Or are you one of the lucky ones? Do you enjoy reading poetry, writing your own poems, and teaching the craft of poetry writing to your students?

Before I teach a lesson on poetry I survey the students to see what they know about poetry in general and how they feel about writing poetry. When I ask young primary students, "What is poetry?" they almost always say that it rhymes. Some of them giggle and say that poetry is funny or like a song. By the time students hit intermediate grades, something unfortunate begins to happen to their attitudes. Only a small number of students in a given classroom admit to enjoying the act of writing poetry. Many students complain that poetry is boring and hard to write. Others openly admit that they do not enjoy poetry. My goal is to change their minds, to show them that writing poetry is easy and fun!

"Noisy" poems possess a kind of magic: there are no rules to follow and any child can experience immediate success. Once your students grasp the hang of writing noisy poems, they may choose to write poetry all year long, as a response to literature, as a means for synthesizing factual information, as a vehicle for writing creatively about any topic or feeling.

Teaching Children to Write Poetry

Students aren't the only ones who don't feel comfortable writing poetry. Teachers often express some of the same inhibitions and concerns. When I ask teachers whether they like to write and teach poetry, I get mixed messages:

✐ *I teach just the forms of poetry like haiku, diamante, limericks, and acrostics.*

✐ *I don't feel comfortable writing poetry in front of my students—or at all.*

✐ *I teach one poetry unit in the spring and that is all I have time for.*

Sometimes the "rules" make poetry seem stifling. Students often have difficulty writing poems that have to rhyme. Think how hard it is to come up with a word that makes sense and that also rhymes. Imagine being a second language learner facing the challenge of filling in words that fit this criterion.

As a child I loved writing poetry but never had any formal instruction in free verse. I still have the little pocket-size poetry notebook with the little red hearts on the cover that I started in fourth grade. The rhyming poems I wrote often started out rather nicely, but I usually ran out of steam. Here is one of my earliest efforts:

> Life is like a river flowing very fast
> One morning you wake up and find the years are past.
> Then you wake up in bed
> And sit up and hit your head.

See what I mean? I have other examples about animals, friendship, and even Creedence Clearwater Revival, my favorite band at the time. All my poems had the same problems with rhyming and word choice. Later I somehow improved my craft and wrote poems (rhyming and non) that were read at family reunions, anniversaries, and funerals.

I guess what I have always liked best about writing poetry is that it allows me to express my feelings freely and in my unique voice. In his book *Poetry Matters* (2002), Ralph Fletcher shares many insights on how poetry allows us to speak to one another's hearts in an intimate way. He says that poetry allows us to feel and empathize with one another. Poetry reflects our inner lives.

What Are Noisy Poems?

Noisy poems are nonrhyming free verse in which "sound," *onomatopoeic*, words (like *crash, eek,* and *oink*) contribute voice and charm. (Later, children can add other literary devices, such as metaphors, similes, personification, repetition, and alliteration.) The key is to write quickly, without worrying about any confining rules. The result? Students write with abandon and surprise themselves and us with their brilliance.

A practical way to motivate children to write quality poetry is to show them poems written by other children. Thanks and credit for this idea go to Regie Routman, who shares this concept, and many poems written by children, in her *Kids' Poems* books (2000). I've used her collections as part of my poetry lessons over the years, and I now have my own large file of student poetry. I project a smattering of examples on transparencies and don't limit myself to the grade level I am teaching. Sixth graders love seeing what little kids write, and younger students feel very grown up seeing the poems of older students. Good poetry is appreciated and celebrated by all. We read each poem chorally two times to appreciate the rhythm and content, and then I ask students to turn and discuss it with a partner. Finally, we chart what we like and notice about the poems.

Figures 3.1 through 3.4 are student-authored poems from a variety of grade levels. They all include a noisy word or two. Some incorporate other literary

Figure 3.1

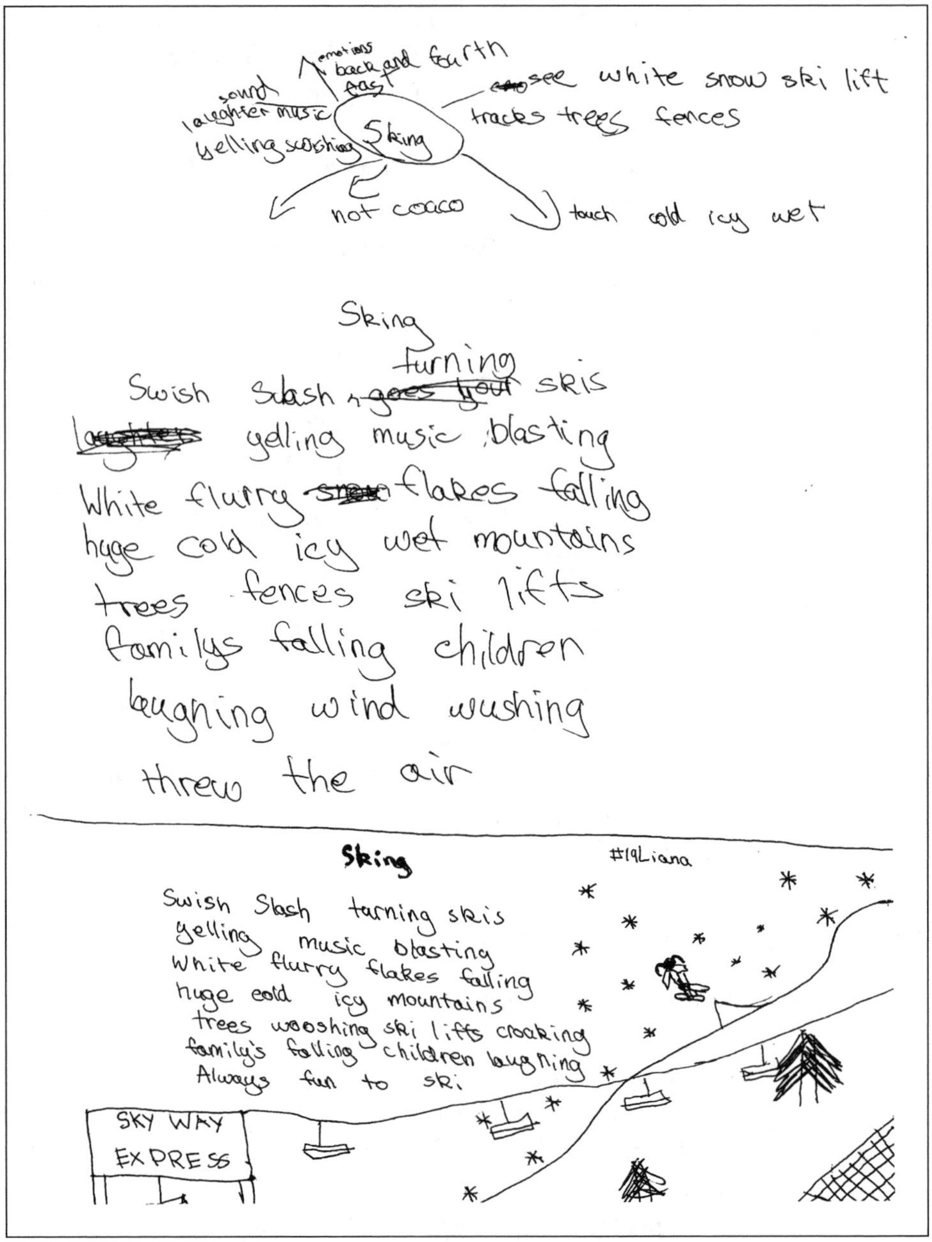

emotions
back and forth
sound
laughter music Skiing see white snow ski lift
yelling scosting tracks trees fences

not cocoa touch cold icy wet

Skiing
turning
Swish slash, goes your skis
laughter yelling music blasting
White flurry snow flakes falling
huge cold icy wet mountains
trees fences ski lifts
familys falling children
laughing wind wushing
threw the air

Skiing   #19 Liana

Swish slash turning skis
yelling music blasting
White flurry flakes falling
huge cold icy mountains
trees wooshing ski lifts croaking
family's falling children laughing
Always fun to ski

SKY WAY
EXPRESS

elements, like metaphor, simile, personification, or alliteration. Think about what you like about each one. What makes it qualify as poetry?

Benefits of Noisy Poems

Free verse offers students many benefits that improve their writing:

- Students write about topics of their choice.

- Students focus on the impact of word choice by using noisy words and other literary techniques that make poems sound interesting.

Figure 3.2

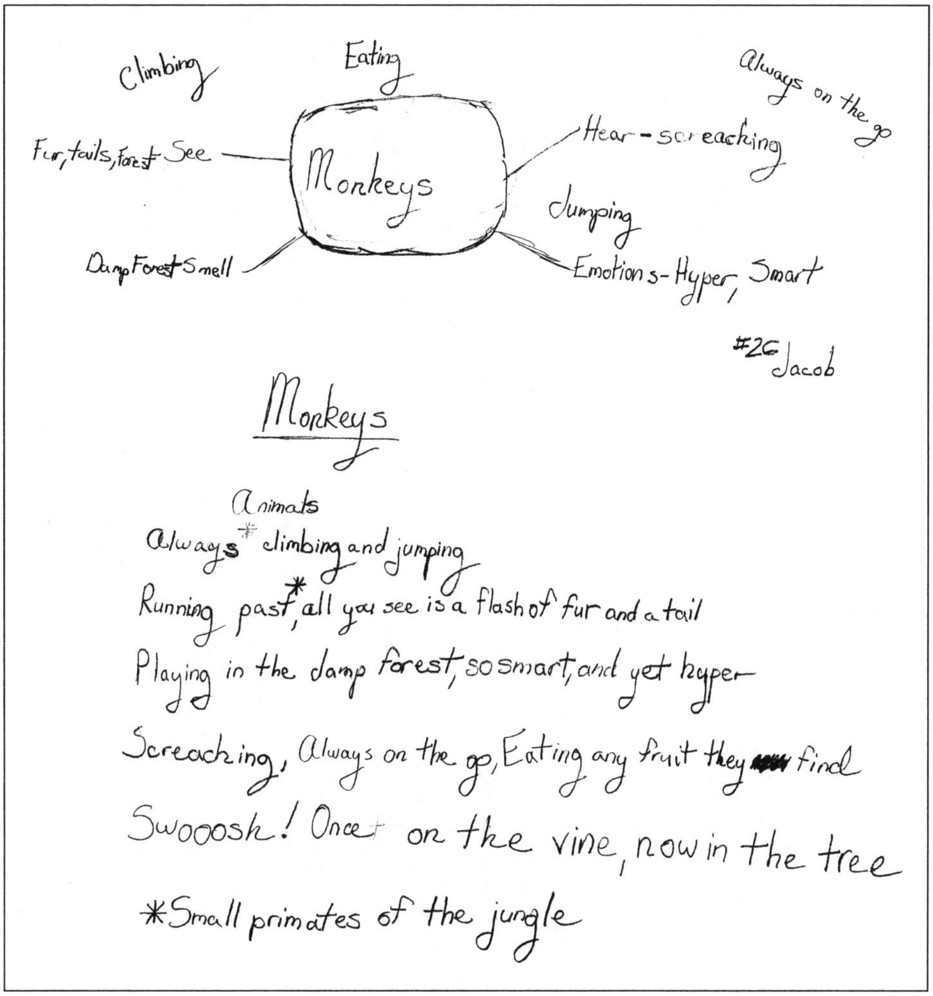

- Students display their personality, or voice, by expressing emotion or humor.

- Reluctant writers are able to avoid being initially bogged down by the details of traditional writing conventions such as sentence structure, periods, and capital letters while focusing on meaning.

At Wilson, an urban school in San Leandro, California, I worked with the first-grade team on some problems the students, many of whom came from homes in which languages other than English were spoken, were having with writing (Oczkus et al. 2006). We noticed that the students wrote listy, dull stories, with every sentence telling a new detail. Students rarely included any emotion or personality in their stilted "and then" strings of sentences. I suggested we teach the students to write noisy free verse in the fall and continue the genre all year long as a way to bring voice and pizzazz to their writing. Our plan included using "skinny paper" (eight-and-a-half-by-eleven-inch sheets cut in half) for poetry writing and regular paper for other types of writing, to remind the children that when they wrote poetry they didn't have to develop full sentences but when they

Figure 3.3

wrote stories and reports they needed to include formal sentences. We conducted guided writing groups and whole-class lessons. Early on we noticed that the students' writing was livelier and more engaging than in years past, and the voices they developed transferred to their other writing. They wrote with more ease and confidence. Poetry showed up in their journals and other free-choice writing. They were hooked!

Poetry as a Response to Literature

Free verse is a quick, easy vehicle for responding to literature. One rainy Sunday evening, my daughter, Rachael, was working diligently to finish a literature response to the *The Golden Goblet* (McGraw 1961). It was getting late and, with only an hour

Figure 3.4

until her bedtime, she asked for my help. She needed an idea for a freewrite or any form of response to end her report. I suggested she try writing a poem about one of the characters in the book. To give her a model, I quickly jotted down one myself about a character in a novel I'd just finished, *Sarah,* by Marek Halter (2004):

Child of Ur

Princess of beauty divine
Her dark secret hidden
Love so deep
She'd do anything
Tortured, tormented, taunted
The childless perfect princess
So divine

Looking at what I'd written, Rachael sighed with relief: "Oh, I just need to repeat a line or even a beginning sound. I can do that." Quickly she began to scribble a draft as I asked her guiding questions:

Ranofer

Tortured, tormented, taunted
Son of Thutra
Abused by his evil half brother Gebu.
Tortured, tormented, taunted
Trapped inside an eggshell that is keeping him from
Pursuing his dream of becoming a master goldsmith.
Tortured, tormented, taunted
Idolizes the master goldsmith, Aau.
Tortured, tormented, taunted
Is startled at finding an ancient golden goblet in
Gebu's forbidden room
Tortured, tormented, taunted.

As you see, she ended up borrowing and (repeating) my alliterative line. Students often mimic our models in the classroom as well. For the next assignment, Rachael wrote a poem on her own, using alliteration but coming up with her own repeating line. The modeling worked! When we model using poetry to reflect on and respond to our reading and guide students in doing so, the result is writing filled with heartfelt words that take them to new levels of understanding. Poetry frees the students to dig deep for thoughts and insights.

Poetry Linked to Report Writing and Nonfiction Topics

Another way to help students synthesize their learning through writing is to give them opportunities to write poems in response to nonfiction topics they've researched. Miss Thrane's first graders had read about rain in guided reading groups. Using their new knowledge about the topic, they then wrote poems in guided writing groups. One group came up with this delightful little poem, each student contributing a line and Miss Thrane brilliantly leading the group in sequencing them:

Rain

"Plink, plink," said the rain.
Splish, splash went the gutter.
Cold, wet, slippery rain dropped.
Whoosh! The wind blows.
The raindrops make plants grow.
Hooray! The sun is back!

Later in the year, we taught these students how to write brief reports that incorporated poems. Then these first graders practiced reading their brief reports and poems to one another in preparation for a writers' tea, at which parents filled the room ready to listen to the proud little writers share their creations. The authors took turns sitting in the author's chair up front. Figure 3.5 is English language learner Jacob's delightful beginning report and corresponding poem about snakes. After Kenny read his spider report and poem, I heard him comment to another child, "I like reading my poem better. It's funnier." What an insight and a gift to know the magic of poetry at such a young age!

Students in Mrs. Arthur's fifth grade were also invited to write poems about topics they'd read about and researched. After researching orca whales and working in a guided writing group, reluctant writer Haley wrote the delightful poem in Figure 3.6 in just a few minutes. She told me she was able to do it so quickly because she already knew so much about these creatures. Her confidence shone! After I've demonstrated writing poetry in a classroom, the teacher will often comment that the struggling and reluctant writers now write more and with greater ease. This is one of the wonderful benefits of noisy poems.

A favorite point that I share with students is the key concept that poems look different from other genres. We also discuss the fact that poetry doesn't follow the rules of conventional writing. I ask them to study poems and search for periods, capital letters, and other conventions. Other than correct spelling (unless writing in a dialect), poets don't follow the rules. I ask classes to chant and repeat after me, "Poetry doesn't follow the rules!" The smiles, chuckles, and sheer joy that permeate the room set the tone for the ideas, voices, and interesting word choices that are unleashed. When it is time to write on their own, the writers jump in with enthusiasm and confidence. This newfound attitude spills over into other kinds of writing, as well.

Figure 3.5

Figure 3.6

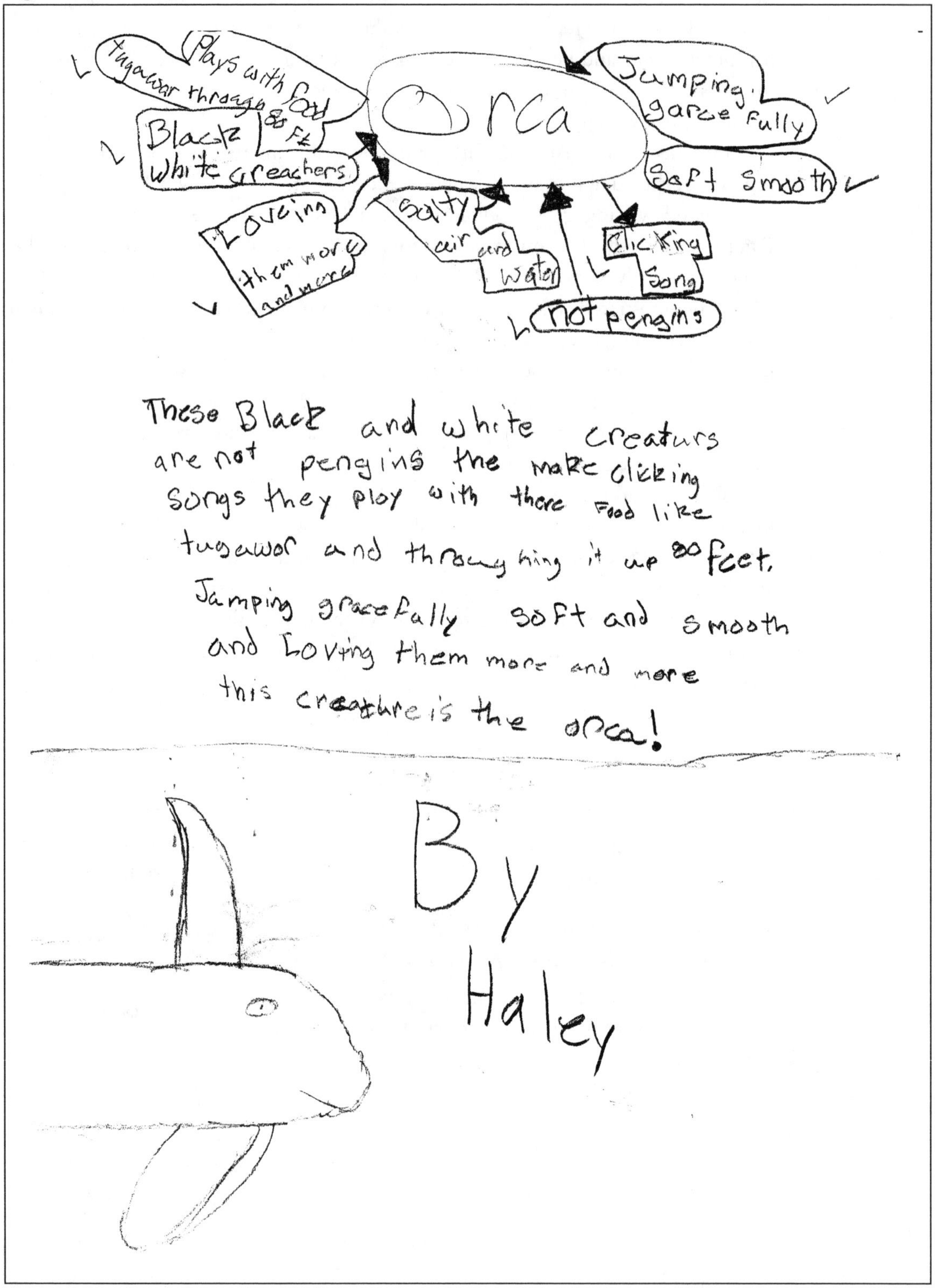
Orca
Plays with food
tugawar throagn 80 Ft
Black white creachers
Loving them more and more
salty air and water
Clicking Song
not pengins
Jumping garcefully
Soft smooth
These Black and white creaturs are not pengins the make clicking songs they ploy with there Food like tugawor and throwghing it up 80 feet. Jamping gracefally soft and smooth and Loving them more and more this creature is the orca!
By Haley

A Noisy Poem Lesson in Action

Halloween is a wonderful time to begin writing noisy poems. All those creepy sounds, like *eek, ooooh,* and *caw,* are a natural inducement. And once you've introduced this type of poetry, you can continue using it all year long as a way to add voice and charm to your students' writing. (This lesson works well not just in first and second grades, but all through elementary school.)

"I flew in on my broom and I'm ready to show you some poetry, haa, haa, hee, hee," I cackle, as I tuck a stray blonde hair under the witch's hat with black stringy hair built in. These first and second graders are spellbound: is it me or a real witch? I wink at Aaron to set him at ease. He smiles with relief.

I begin by asking the class to brainstorm a list of noisy Halloween words. Once the list is generated, I show examples of noisy Halloween poems some of my former students have written. The children notice that the poems are short, sometimes funny, and often repeat a word or line. Next I create a web of Halloween words and noises at the top of a projected transparency. All eyes are on me as I begin to write my own poem below the web. I think aloud, telling the students I'd like to try repeating a line or word in my poem. Here's what I come up with:

The Scary Witch

Hee, hee, hee
The scary witch
flies
Hee, hee, hee
she haunts the dark night sky
with her broom
Hee, hee, hee

Next I invite a student, Grace, up to the overhead projector to "help" model how to write a poem. I guide her as she writes:

Bat

Flap, flap, flap
The black bat flies
through the scary sky
Flap, flap, flap

When I invite the students to respond to this quick little poem, they say they like the noisy word *flap* and the repetition.

The little band of students seated cross-legged in front of me on the rug has paid close attention to the lesson and they are ready to write on their own. I ask them to turn to a partner and tell what Halloween "things" and corresponding noises will be in their poem. As I hand out pieces of paper, I ask them to stand up, face the class, and tell us a noisy word they plan to repeat in their poem. Then all pencils hit the unlined paper with abandon. Circulating through the room, I stop at each child's desk. I read aloud now and then from a poem and ask the class to listen to examples of wonderful scary noises, funny lines, repetition, and other interesting examples. We end the lesson with students taking turns reading their poems to the class for rounds of applause and for loads of compliments. It is time for me to leave. I tell them I need to find my black cat and get ready for Halloween. They giggle and wave good-bye, and I feel sure they will not soon forget how to write a noisy poem.

After school I type up their masterpieces, and the next day they illustrate their poems (see Figures 3.7 through 3.10). The hallway outside the classroom becomes a gallery where the whole school can see their work. In the weeks to come their teacher will help them write poems in guided lessons with smaller groups. The students are on their way to becoming poets!

Scaffolded lesson

SCAFFOLDED **Noisy Poem Lessons**

Objectives

- Study examples of noisy poems written by published and student authors.

- Brainstorm ideas for a noisy poem on a web or in a list.

- Discuss with partners noises to be used in the poem.

- Write a noisy poem that repeats noises, words, or phrases.

- Incorporate other literary elements, such as metaphors, similes, personification, and alliteration.

- Focus on word choice and voice.

Figure 3.7

Figure 3.8

OOOOOOOOh!
Red ghost.
Boo! Black spider.
Haha I'm gonna get
you! Blue Witch.
Whoosh! Whoosh! Spooky!
Yellow Pumpkin.
Halloween noises.

Identify Examples

- *Show students a variety of poems written by adult authors as well as children* (feel free to use ones from this book; additional examples are shown in Figures 3.11 through 3.15). Don't worry about grade level. Students learn from reading all types of poems by all types of poets.

- *Ask students open-ended questions about these poems.* Have them tell you what they like or notice about each poem after they have first shared their ideas with a partner. You may want to give students their own copy so that they can underline or highlight favorite parts and words.

- *Begin a What Makes a Great Noisy Poem rubric or list.* As students name what they like about the poems, list their responses on the board or a chart. Some of their ideas might include:
  - Noisy poems are skinny.
  - Noisy poems are sometimes scary or funny.
  - Noisy poems repeat words, sounds, or lines.

✐ Noisy poems some times use made-up words to describe sounds.

Appendix D offers a sample rubric for noisy poems.

cool
tools

✐ *Introduce cool tools.* Have students place sticky notes next to examples of noisy poem elements. Make copies of poems and let students highlight or underline interesting words or other teaching points. Invite students to come up to student poems that are projected on transparencies and underline favorite parts and words.

✐ *Assess student progress.* Do the students need more examples of noisy poems? Can they verbalize their observations? Have students turn in their highlighted or underlined examples. What kinds of examples do they need now?

Figure 3.9

Boo a green head.
A black cat stretching through the hall.
Whoosh goes the wind on a black spooky night.

Modeling

✐ *Brainstorm your own noisy poem.* (See Figures 3.16 and 3.17).

  ✐ Write on the whiteboard, a piece of chart paper, or a projected transparency. Use the first quarter or third of the space. (Define the space by folding the paper to form a crease or draw a horizontal line across the page.)
  ✐ Brainstorm ideas and related noisy words.
  ✐ Think aloud, inviting students to ask questions that will help you add details to your web.
  ✐ Include all the senses (sight, hearing, touch, taste, and smell) and emotional reactions.
  ✐ Include "like what" metaphors and similes.

Figure 3.10

Owl   black   broom

blackcat   Happy   Screech
hee   Halliween
                 wichis   flap

Happy, Halliween wichis
Hee! Hee! screech! screech!
goes the sceery black witch
The witch flies
through the sceery Blue
sky! vroom! vroom! vroom!
Hee! Hee! screech! screech!
crash! trip! stumbl!

By Rebecca

Figure 3.11

#13 Hank

Crackle, Crackle hums the flare
blazing colors of orange and red
with smoke blowing and clouding in the wind
cozy and peaseful like everlasting serenity
excitement flows and fills my body with warmth
only wishing wishing it would stay
blowing whisps and burning
with embers fading and smoke flying
Crackle, Crackle hums the flare

Figure 3.12

October 31st

Perched on a hill
Quiet little town
On Halloween Eve
"Woooh!" wind blows ominously
Leaves stirring in street
Awakening call answered by
Flapping black bats
Creaking wooden posts
Rattling roaming skeletons
Stomping morbid mummies
Ghastly groaning ghosts
Hissing black cats
"Auwh" howls wolf
As cloud covers moon
Silencing again the night

Jason

Figure 3.13

Pencil Sharpener

Annoying loud buzzing sound,
From a little black box.

A pencil in it's little mouth,
A tail in it's power charge.

The poor little yellow fellow
The little black box
rips of it's flesh.
Down into a stomach of clear despair.
The little sound that angers me
while I try to consintrate.
Annoying loud buzzing sound
From a little black box.

Michelle

Figure 3.14

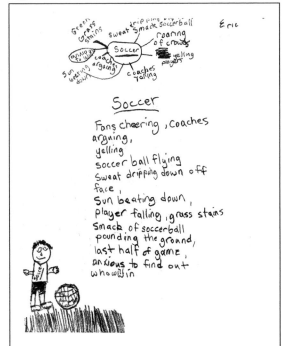

Soccer

Fans cheering, coaches
arguing,
yelling
soccer ball flying
Sweat dripping down off
face,
Sun beating down,
player falling, grass stains
Smack of soccerball
pounding the ground,
last half of game,
anxious to find out
who will win

Figure 3.15

When the music plays I feel it moving through
my body
my muscles let go as I move across the
floor in graceful steps
hear the beat

boom
tap
tap
boom
bye bye I say to my worries and bad
feelings as they float away with every
step, bye bye
hear the beat
boom
tap
tap
boom
opening my mind
letting my emotions set sail on a
musical joy ride
so long I say to my bad feelings
bye bye
hear the beat
boom
tap
tap
boom
I am alone It's just me and the music

55

🖎 *Write your noisy poem* (Figures 3.16 and 3.17).

  🖎 First tell students the focus. You can say something like, "I will try to re-peat an interesting noisy word throughout the poem. Also, I will include at least two metaphors."

  🖎 Talk as you write each sentence. Pretend to get stuck. Scratch words out and rewrite as you go.

  🖎 Reread aloud to see how it sounds. Tell students that good writers reread as they revise and think of what to write next.

  🖎 *Add to the rubric.* Ask students to tell what they think is important or what they liked about your modeling.

🖎 *Introduce cool tools.* Throughout the lesson stop and check student understanding by way of thumbs-up or thumbs-down signals. Ask, *Does this word sound right here? Read it with me. What do you like about this?*

🖎 *Assess student progress.* Are students ready to write on their own after seeing you model? Are they in the "mood" to write? Do they need a shared writing step or can you jump to independent writing?

Shared Writing

🖎 *Invite students help you write a noisy poem.* Let students to suggest a few lines.

OR

🖎 *Encourage a volunteer to write a sample in front of the class.* Have other students in the class suggest noisy words and interesting repetitions. (If the student is a reluctant writer or English language learner, you may want to serve as scribe as the student dictates.)

🖎 *Assess student progress.* How did students do during discussions? Are they ready to write? Do you need to call up a small group and guide them while they write their poems? Would some students benefit from writing a guided poem as a group?

Figure 3.16

Hee, hee, hee!
The scary witch flies
She haunts the night, dark sky with her broom
Her skinny black cat meows all through the night.
Hee, hee, hee!

Figure 3.17

My Noisy Poem

Name: _____   Date: _____

Fold your paper on the line. Brainstorm ideas for your poem first.

My Brainstorm Web

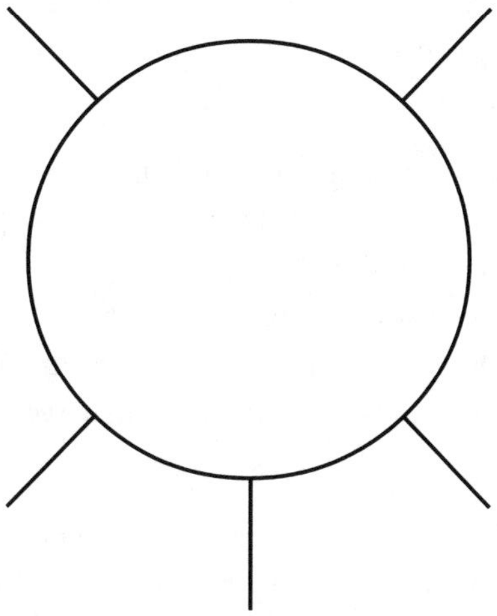

Write your noisy poem here.

Title _____

Guided Writing

- *Implement guided writing during a whole-class lesson.*
  - Meet with table groups.
  - Rotate to tables as students work on their individual poems.
  - Have each student at the table read her or his piece aloud. Ask the other group members to write compliments and suggestions for changes on sticky notes and give them to the writer. (With younger children, you might write what the group members say and hand the notes to the writer.)

- *Implement guided writing during writing workshop.*
  - Invite students who wish to write noisy poems to work with you in a temporary poets' club.
  - Over several sessions, have students each write their own poems, conferring with you and the rest of the group as they go.
  - Ask several volunteers to share their work at the end of writing workshop.

- *Implement guided writing during guided reading.*
  - Pass out sentence strips or a similar cool tool to group members.
  - Ask each student to write a line for a noisy poem that will capture an incident or a character in the book the group has read.
  - Guide individual students as they work.
  - Use a pocket chart to sequence the lines in an order that makes sense. (The group may want to add lines or words between the strips.)
  - Read the poem as a group or have each student read the line she or he contributed.

- *Assess student progress.* Can students now work independently, or do they need to continue to meet in a group to finish their work?

Independent Writing

- *Remind students to refer to the rubric or list, your model, and the shared poem for guidance.*

- *Circulate through the room.* Prompt individual students as they write. Occasionally ask for everyone's attention and read aloud a word, phrase, or entire poem that illustrates one of your teaching points. (Be sure to ask permission to read a student's poem aloud before doing so. Some students may feel uncomfortable about sharing their work.) These "FYIs" provide just the right amount of modeling for writers who might be stuck. (The young poets will soon beg you to read their writing aloud.)

- *Assess student progress.* Do students apply what they have learned from the modeled and shared writing lessons in their own writing? Do they need to return to a guided group format?

Figure 3.18

Possible Noisy Poem Minilessons Focusing on the Six Traits

Ideas

- Noisy poems can be about anything. Keep a running class list of possible topics.

- Try getting away from clichéd general topics like love and stars. Instead, use things like shoelaces, the last of the cereal floating in milk, and almost being late. (Fletcher, 2002)

Word Choice

- Word choice is critical in writing noisy poems. Ask students to hunt for words they've repeated. Do they want to keep them the same for effect or change words to make the poem stronger?

- What are some interesting noisy words? Do the words students choose relate to the senses? the emotions?

- Have students try alliteration, or the repetition of beginning sounds in a line of text.

- Do your students have too many noisy words in their poems? Is just one noisy word okay?

Organization

- Ask students how noisy poems are organized.

- Show students how some free verse poetry is shaped.

- Ask students how noisy poems begin. Experiment with a repeating word, noise, line, or verse.

- Try beginning and ending noisy poems with the same line.

- Some noisy poems contain a surprise ending. Ask how students can make the ending a surprise.

Sentence Fluency

- Students read noisy poems aloud. Are some sentences short and others long?

- What is the difference between a poem and a story? Does a poem always have sentences? Are phrases okay? Why?

- Can all the lines in a noisy poem begin in the same way? How do poets break sentence rules when they write?

- Can one word stand on a line alone? Have students try it.

- Read noisy poems aloud and decide where line breaks make sense. Try not to make conventional sentences but rather find other ways to divide up lines.

Voice

Invite students to:

- Take the point of view of a character or object.

- "Talk" to the subject or topic of a poem.

- Add a humorous or silly noisy word.

- Reveal their feelings about a topic with show-not-tell phrases.

Conventions

- Poets break the rules. Tell two ways they do this. Discuss.

- Compare the conventions in a story, a report, and a poem, and how they differ.

- Check poems for spelling. What if a noisy word is made up? How can it be spelled it so readers can pronounce it?

- Noisy poetry is all about fluency; no red marks!

Guided Conferring

✐ *Have students read their work to each other in small groups,* using the rubric as a guideline for compliments and suggestions.

✐ *Set up a gallery tour.* Have students leave their poem on their desk along with a piece of paper that has three columns labeled Reader's Name/Compliment/ Question. On your signal, have students move quietly from desk to desk reading one another's poems. Since writing a response to every poem will take too long, ask students to fill out the form only when you say, "Take a minute to write about this one." Do this three or four times. When students return to their desks and read the comments, they may choose to revise their work.

✐ *Meet with table groups after a gallery tour.* Invite one student to read his or her poem, along with the suggestions and compliments. Guide the group in helping the writer rewrite, then let the remaining group members rewrite their poems with help from the other members.

✐ *Conduct a hunt-and-share.* Choose one element in the noisy poem rubric, such as incorporating similes. Ask students to find an example in their own work and share the example with a partner or their tablemates. Choose one child to share their example with the whole class. Select another teaching point for students to hunt for and share.

Discussion Questions

1. Do your students like writing poetry? Why or why not? Do you like teaching poetry? Do you enjoy writing or reading poetry yourself? Why or why not?

2. What are some problems you encounter when teaching poetry? Why is rhyming so difficult for students?

3. How do noisy poems compare with other types of poetry you've seen or taught? What is similar or different? What are the advantages of noisy poems?

4. Show your students some poems from this chapter. Why are student samples such powerful models? How do your students respond? How can you collect more samples from your own classroom and other classrooms in the school?

5. Noisy poetry lessons can include any or all the scaffolded steps. If you had to select just two, which would you pick and why?

Try It in Your Classroom

✐ Lead your class outside into the yard or playground. Have students stand in a circle and close their eyes. Tell them what you hear. For example: "I hear birds chirping. The noisy words I'd choose for my poem are *chirp, chirp* or *tweet, tweet*. I hear the wind. I think I'll say *whoosh* for that." Ask students to share what they hear. Return to the classroom and model how to write a brief noisy poem based on the sounds you heard outside. Invite students to write poems at their tables or on their own. Evaluate how things went. What will you add when you repeat the lesson? (This is a great introductory lesson for children of any age.)

✐ Share student poems on transparencies with your class. (Use poems from this chapter or your own students' pieces.) How does this make the lesson more effective? Make individual copies of the poems for your students. Invite them to highlight interesting words and phrases. How does this help your students?

✐ Write noisy poems on a variety of subjects. Write poems as a response to literature and as a response to a nonfiction topic or report. Discuss how each lesson went. How does writing in response to reading help students comprehend?

✐ Bring some of your students' noisy poems to a meeting of your colleagues. Study the patterns. What are students doing well? Do you see evidence of voice? What do they need to work on? Use copies of poems from a variety of grade levels in your next lessons. Students delight in seeing the work of other students in their school.

Chapter Four

What's Your Story? Personal Narrative and Weekend Webs

Writing is a memory on paper.
—Audrey

Rethinking a Writing Tradition

Every Monday students everywhere file into their classrooms, pull out their weekend news journals, and begin writing about the events of their two-day break from school. The entries are usually a laundry list of movies, cartoons, visitors, play dates, junk food, mundane chores, and occasional outings. The "and thens" flow as students spin out the thread of events that make up their lives. As the parent of three children myself, I've saved these precious records as a sort of family diary. I'm glad we have them as precious keepsakes. Sometimes they even reveal secrets:

Weekend News

by Bryan Oczkus, Second Grader

On the weekend I had a baseball game. I read a book. I helped Dad sand a picnic table. After that my mom made us go furnurshur shoping. Theres nothgin boringer then furnurshur shoping. On Sunday we went to church. We made lunch and dinner for Mom. I played a game of Yahtzee aginst my mom. I won. After that my mom got me new shoes. That was my weekend.

Weekend news occupies a dear and revered spot in the writing traditions of many teachers. I am not suggesting that we toss out something so many students, teachers, and even parents look forward to. But maybe we can build on this popular writing activity to improve student writing. Here are some of the problems teachers readily express when asked what they don't like about weekend news:

- *Students don't stick to a topic and elaborate with detail.*

- *Every sentence is a new idea as students race to cram in all of their weekend events.*

- *Sentences tend to be boring as students link together an endless litany of "and thens."*

- *Some students don't do much over the weekend except watch television or play video games and they don't have much to write about.*

- *Weekend news takes up time and I have so much to teach.*

- *Many students dislike writing their weekend news.*

I began to wonder if teachers could retain the concept of recounting one's weekend on paper while at the same time teaching some valuable writing strategies and skills. The teachers I work with and I began to experiment with a powerful alternative called weekend webs.

What Are Weekend Webs?

A weekend web lets students tell all about their weekend and then zero in on one specific event or idea to write about in detail. The detailed piece is very brief but well written; it uses the particular writing technique the class is focusing on at the time, such as using sensory details, writing an interesting beginning, or adding dialogue.

The two-step process begins with brainstorming the weekend's happenings. Students have three to five minutes in which to scribble down as much as they can remember about their Friday-to-Sunday respite. Then they zero in on one of the bubbles or ideas on their web and spend another two minutes adding descriptive details. The last few minutes are spent writing one or two short paragraphs about the chosen event or activity. Here's how it plays out:

- The student brainstorms and reflects on his or her weekend activities.

- The student selects only one idea or event from the web and adds detail to that part of the web.

- The students discusses the idea or event with a partner, who asks good questions and probes for details. (Younger students may even draw an illustration before writing their piece.)

- The student writes a brief but detailed paragraph or two describing or recounting the idea or event.

Figure 4.1 shows Clayton's overall web, the details he added to the baseball brainstorm, and the piece he wrote.

Benefits of Weekend Webs

The benefits of a weekend web are many, for both teachers and students:

- Students still get to record all their weekend events on paper but in the more manageable form of a graphic web.

- Students have time every week to write a focused, detailed first draft about a topic they care about.

- Teachers model powerful writing techniques and skills.

- Students are freed from the tyranny of conventions and can concentrate on fluency.

- The best drafts may be polished and published.

Figure 4.1

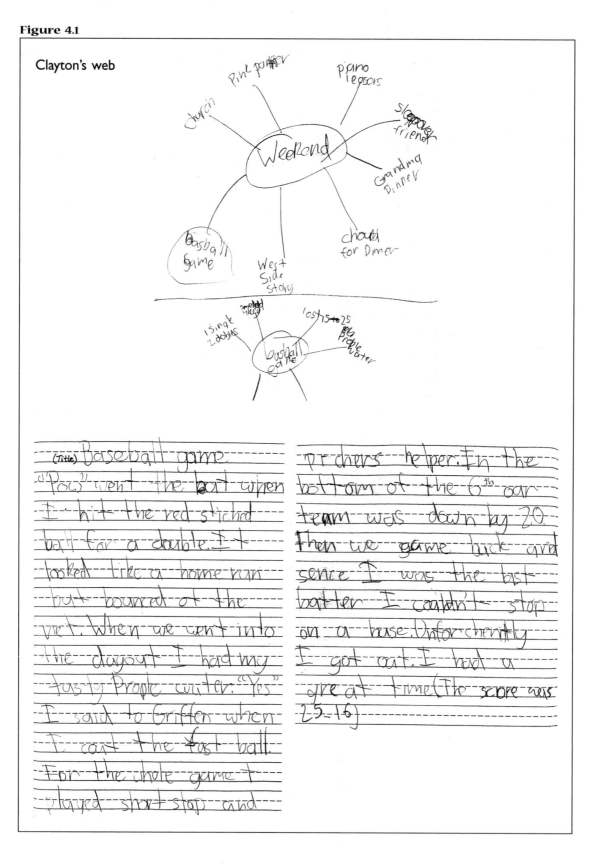

Clayton's web

(Title) Baseball game
"Pow" went the bat when
I hit the red stiched
ball for a double. It
looked like a home run
but bounced of the
wall. When we went into
the dugout I had my
tusty People writer. "Yes"
I said to Griffen when
I cat the fast ball.
For the whole game I
played short stop and

pitchers helper. In the
bottom of the 6th oar
team was down by 20.
Then we game bick and
sence I was the last
batter I couldn't stop
on a base. Unforchently
I got out. I had a
great time (The score was
25-16)

Writing Inch by Inch

Have you noticed that students love hearing about our personal lives, even when we mention mundane things like our car or toilet breaking down or our dog getting sick? They are all ears. This makes the weekend web great fun to model. For example, each Monday one third-grade teacher celebrated the predictability and even dullness of her simple but relaxing weekends. Her class thought she was hilarious. They began to remind her to include routines if she forgot them ("You forgot your Saturday morning double vanilla latte!").

The fact that you can model any writing skill or technique you want is the beauty of this lesson. If you are teaching how to begin a story or personal narrative, for example, you might begin your piece with a quote or description and have students do the same in their own pieces. Or you might focus on sentence variety, beginning every sentence differently. You can model (and have students incorporate) any of the six traits or any specific skill your students need to learn. The sky's the limit.

For many students, writing means staring at a blank intimidating paper, not knowing where to start. Weekend webs teach students not to become overwhelmed but to focus on a bit at a time, select a tiny event or idea to describe, and make that one topic interesting. This focus is just what they need in order to understand how to develop detail in their writing. I love Anne Lamott's idea, described in her book *Bird by Bird* (1994), of writing inch by inch: when you focus on a little piece of what you want to write and say as much about it as you can fit into a one-inch frame, writing is easy. Sometimes I bring in a tiny one-inch frame I bought at the dollar store and use it when I model.

Here are some examples of one-inch writing that I've modeled for students:

- The squirrel running across our deck so joyfully that morning.

- The dishwasher backing up and forcing us to do dishes by hand all weekend, which reminded me of my childhood when that was my job with my sister—and was fun.

- The daffodils signaling springtime in our yard and neighborhood.

- Making a cake with my daughter.

Weekend Webs in Action

Turning Out Storytellers

Mrs. Carpenter already does a marvelous job with her traditional weekend news. Instead of asking students to list their weekend activities and string them into a recounting of the two days, she has taught them to select just one event to write about. She and I decide that weekend webs will provide even more support as students focus on developing their ideas.

"What are the ingredients for a good story?" I ask the eager second graders. They raise their hands and throw out ideas, like interesting characters, a problem, a solution, and an ending. Several of the children add that details are important in stories. We briefly discuss stories they've recently read as a class.

I tell them that every day their lives include interesting events that make wonderful stories. I also let them know that today they will begin writing quick paragraphs that are really stories about something that happened to them over the weekend and that if they choose to, they can add to their piece and make it longer during writing workshop.

Next I brainstorm my weekend on a projected transparency, thinking aloud as I go: "I went to a musical at the high school on Friday night." "I tripped during my step aerobics class on Saturday morning." "It was very warm on Sunday afternoon, and my kids had a water fight!" (See Figure 4.2).

Figure 4.2

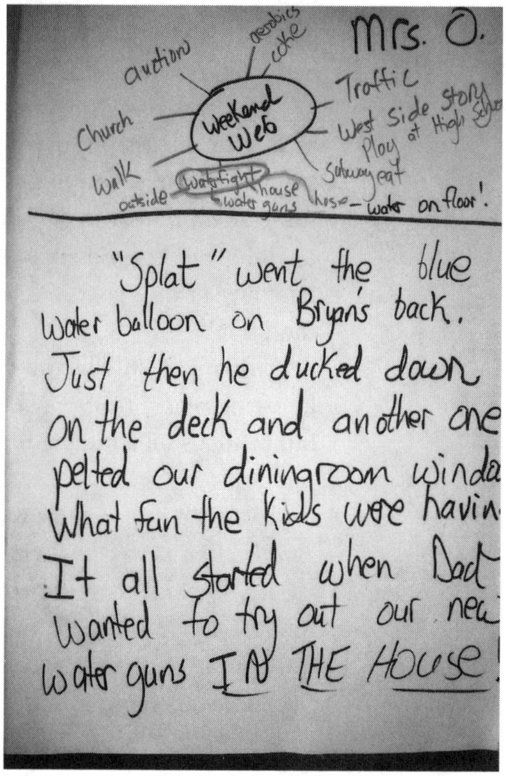

Then I make my hand into a fist, hold it up to my eye, and open it slightly to form a "topic tube" I can look through. "Let me look for an idea that would make a good story." I think aloud about each item and decide to write about the water fight. "What details do I know about it?" I return to the web and add details as I describe to the students what happened. They giggle when I tell them that my husband started it all.

Finally I begin writing, reminding myself aloud that I want to make sure I tell it like a story:

"Splat," went the blue water balloon on Bryan's back. Just then he ducked down on the deck and another one pelted into our dining room window. What fun the kids were having! It all started when Dad wanted to try out our new toy water guns IN THE HOUSE! Yikes! So, I kicked them all out after the floors were soaked with puddles everywhere. Then the neighbor kids wanted to join in the wild, wet fun. Everyone grabbed balloons, water guns, and hoses. Once they ran out of balloons, they used sandwich baggies. Thank goodness it was time for dinner! Everyone was completely soaked!

When I finish I ask the students to turn and tell a partner what they like about my piece. This is what they come up with:

Details—lots of them.

We can picture it in our heads.

It was funny.

Noisy words—the story began with one.

Figure 4.3

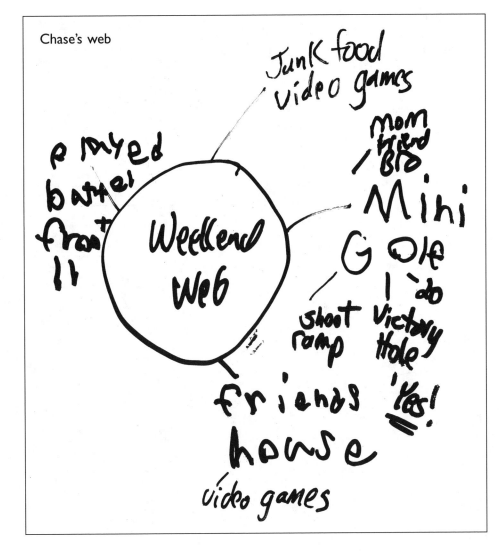

Chase's web

Next I ask who is willing to come up and create a web of his or her weekend on a projected transparency. Chase volunteers. He writes some of the words, and to speed up the process I write some that he dictates (see Figure 4.3). Then he invites students to ask him questions about his focus topic, a game of miniature golf.

By this time we have used up most of the writing period. While I circulate, the students only have time to web their weekends and select a topic on which to focus. Not getting as far as I think I will always makes me feel a bit guilty, but I remind myself that this is a new process. I will move on to independent writing and offer some guided writing support during the next class period.

The next day I review how to write a piece using details, dialogue, and noisy words—the story elements Mrs. Carpenter has been focusing on in writing workshop—and the students begin writing.

We follow this process of modeling, sharing, and guiding for several months and the students' weekend webs improve. Their writing begins to take on voice and personality (see the two students' work in Figures 4.4 and 4.5).

Figure 4.4

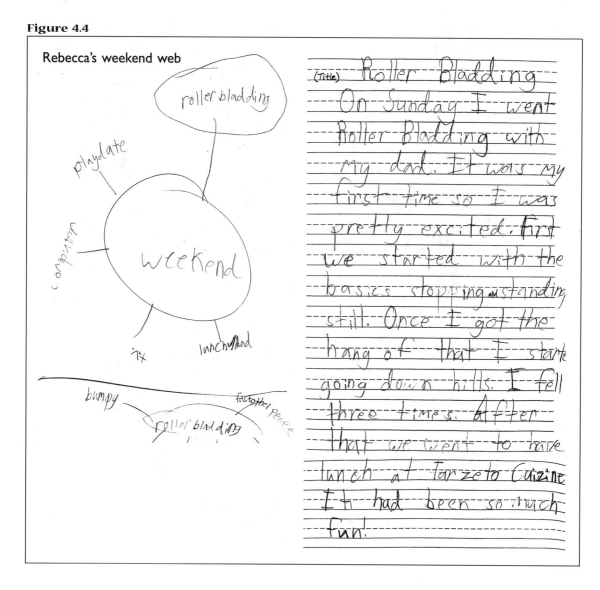

Rebecca's weekend web

(Title) Roller Bladding

On Sunday I went Roller Bladding with my dad. It was my first time so I was pretty excited. First we started with the basics stopping and standing still. Once I got the hang of that I started going down hills. I fell three times. After that we went to have lunch at Tarzeto Cuizine It had been so much fun.

Teaching Craft and Skills

The weekend web is a versatile tool you can use to introduce or reinforce any writing skill within the context of student-centered topics. Robyn Arthur uses weekend webs and journals all year long in her combined fourth-fifth grade, incorporating the skills and strategies that make up the author's craft. After webbing the weekend and choosing one event to write about (Figure 4.6), the students write their narratives, making sure to incorporate the strategy or skill that is being focused on in that particular session. Mrs. Arthur encourages them to try different beginnings, use dialogue, express feelings, and incorporate vivid verbs and adjectives. Patrick's web and narrative in Figure 4.7 was written during a class in which Mrs. Arthur asked her students to focus on alternate beginnings, the sounds or noises they heard in relation to the web entry, and vivid details. Hannah's web and narrative (see Figure 4.8) was written during a class on incorporating dialogue and details.

Figure 4.5

B's weekend web

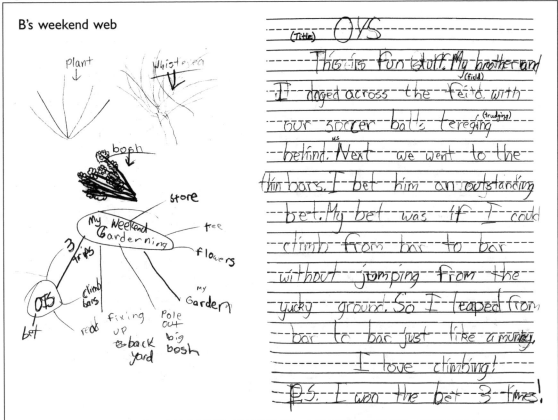

Figure 4.6

Figure 4.7

Patrick's web

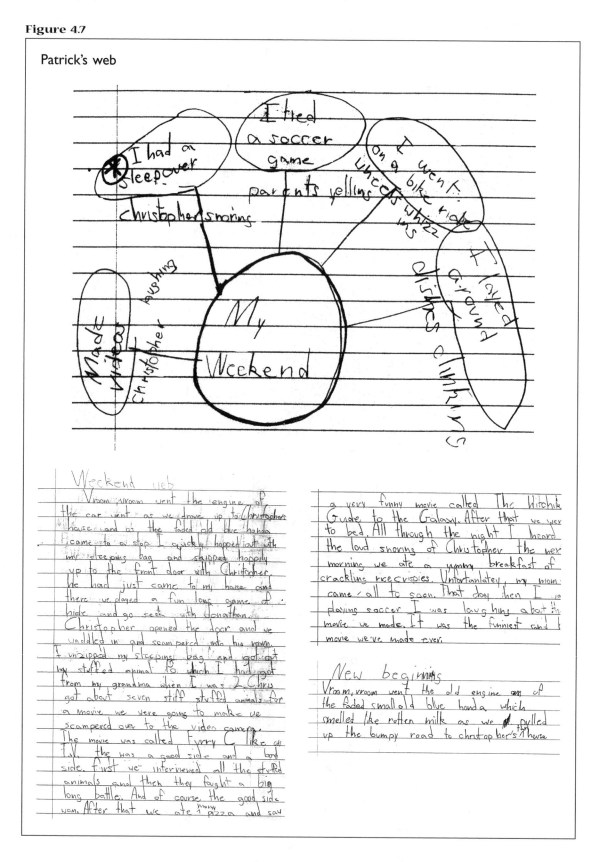

Weekend web

Vroom, vroom went the engine of the car went as we drove up to Christophers house, and as the faded old blue honda came to a stop I quickly hopped out with my sleeping bag and skipped happily up to the front door with Christoher. He had just came to my house and there we played a fun long game of hide and go seek with Jonathan. Christopher opened the door and we waddled in and scampered into his room. I unzipped my sleeping bag and got out my stuffed animal B. which I had got from my grandma when I was 2. Chris got about seven stiff stuffed animals for a movie we were going to make we scampered over to the video camera. The movie was called Furry C like on TV. the was a good side and a bad side. First we interviewed all the stuffed animals and then they fought a big long battle. And of course the good side won. After that we ate yummy pizza and saw

a very funny movie called The Hitchhike Guide to the Galaxy. After that we wen to bed. All through the night I heard the loud snoring of Christopher the nex morning we ate a yummy breakfast of crackling rice crispies. Unfortanlatey, my mom came all to soon. That day when I wa playing soccer I was laughing about th movie we made. It was the funniest and movie we've made ever.

New beginnings

Vroom, vroom went the old engine of the faded small old blue honda which smelled like rotten milk as we pulled up the bumpy road to christopher's house

Figure 4.8

Hannah's weekend web

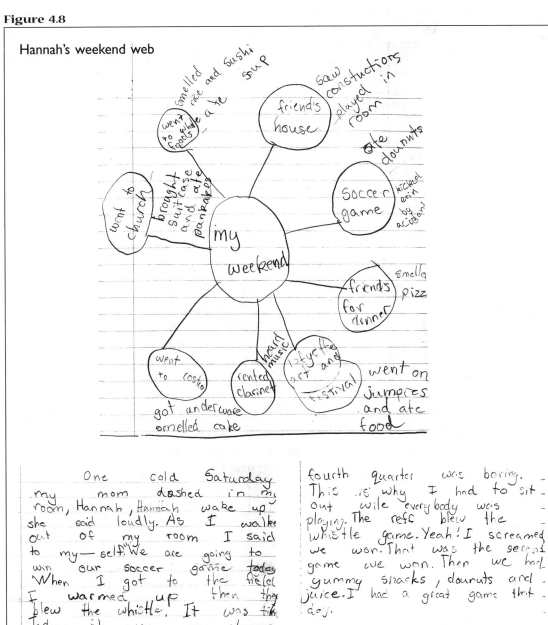

One cold Saturday my mom dashed in my room, Hannah, Hannah wake up she said loudly. As I walke out of my room I said to my—self "We are going to win our soccer game today When I got to the field I warmed up then they blew the whistle! It was tim today it was my chance to prove We could win! I was forward in the first quarter. Boom! I kicked a goal. Score! Everyone shouted you scored a goal In the second quarter I was gaaly the other team smached a goal right at me I caught it I was so realived. It was the third quarter I was mid I was chasing after the ball I soored again. The

fourth quarter was boring. This is why I had to sit out wile everybody was playing. The reff blew the whistle game. Yeah! I screamed we won. That was the second game we won. Then we had yummy snacks, dounuts and juice. I had a great game that day.

Scaffolded lesson

SCAFFOLDED Weekend Web Lessons

Weekend webs and journal entries are often the focus of a fifteen- to thirty-minute writing period on Mondays, a kind of quickwrite to promote fluency. They may also be spread over several days, especially when they are first introduced. After the process is familiar and routine, briefly model your teaching point, provide the shared and guided writing opportunities you think are needed, and let the students dig in (Figure 4.9). Weekend webs should be quick, fun, and easy.

Objectives

- ✐ Brainstorm weekend activities on a web or in a list.

- ✐ Discuss with a partner the topic chosen to elaborate on.

- ✐ Write a brief, focused piece incorporating the strategy or writing skill that was taught in the session.

Identifying Examples

You may not need to use this step every week; it maybe most useful only when you want to teach a new skill, or when examples are readily available. You might also share examples from books throughout the week *after* the lesson. For example, you might model using dialogue in your weekend web piece; then, during the week, you and your students could identify how authors use dialogue in their pieces and the following Monday you could share examples using dialogue and ask students to incorporate dialogue again into their journal entries.

- ✐ *Decide on a skill or strategy you wish to teach or reinforce.* Select one you need to teach based on either student needs or your curriculum. Some examples include using dialogue, onomatopoeia, or sensory details; piquing reader interest; varying the beginnings of sentences; adding detail; displaying emotion or humor; and paying attention to interesting verbs or adjectives.

- ✐ *State the objective or purpose of the skill or strategy.* Say something like, *When good writers write they use [different verbs] to help them [sound more interesting and give the reader a strong visual picture].*

- ✐ *Find examples.* Select a variety of examples of the targeted skill or strategy from books or other texts. It is especially powerful to use samples of other students' weekend journal entries. (Feel free to show your students the ones in this book.)

- ✐ *Begin a rubric.* Invite students to turn first to a partner and then discuss with the class what they think is important to remember about using the targeted skill or strategy. Appendix D shows a sample weekend web rubric.

- ✐ *Introduce cool tools.* Have students use sticky notes to mark examples of the targeted skill or strategy.

- ✐ *Assess student progress.* Do the students need more examples of this skill or strategy? Can they verbalize their observations? Have students turn in their highlighted or underlined examples.

Figure 4.9

Over the Weekend

Name: _____   Date: _____

My Weekend Web

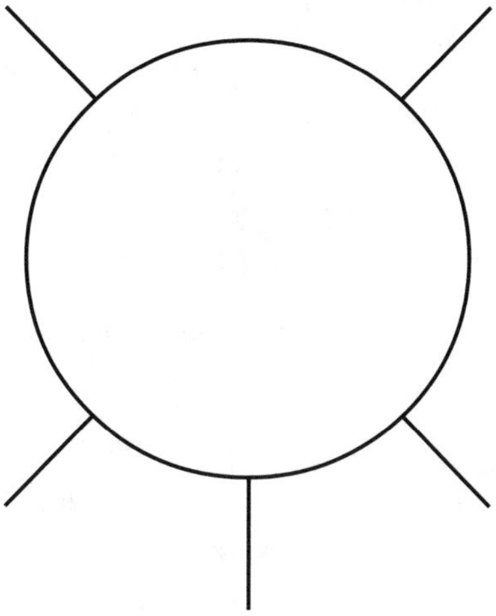

(fold here)

My Topic Is:

_____

_____

_____

_____

_____

_____

_____

_____

_____

_____

_____

_____

_____

Modeling

Modeling is the most powerful portion of any lesson. Try to do it as often as possible.

✐ *Brainstorm your own weekend web.* Write on either the whiteboard, chart paper, or a projected transparency. Tell students that good writers often write about their own experiences.

✐ *Select one of your entries and tell why you are choosing it.* If you wish, roll a piece of paper into a "topic tube" and scan your web with it. (See Figure 4.6.) Once you select your topic, think aloud about it: *I have more to say about this. This was really funny [interesting, sad]. This is an image I want to remember in my mind. This was so special I want to remember it in detail.*

✐ *Begin webbing ideas and details around your selected topic.* Invite students to ask you questions that will elicit details.

✐ *Write your weekend journal entry.* Tell students what the focus skill is today: *I am writing about the flowers in my yard, so I will use sensory details to help the reader make a picture in his or her head.* Talk as you write each sentence. Pretend to get stuck. Visualize details as a way to remember them.

✐ *Reread your own writing.* Tell students that good writers reread as they revise and think of what to write next.

✐ *Add to the rubric.* Ask students to tell what they think is important or what they liked about your modeling.

✐ *Introduce cool tools.* Check student understanding via thumbs-up or thumbs-down signals: *Did I include enough detail here? Can you see a picture in your head? Do I need to use another verb here?* Volunteers might act out parts of your piece.

✐ *Assess student progress.* Are students ready to write on their own? Are they in the "mood" to write? Do they need a shared writing step or can you jump to independent writing?

Shared Writing

✐ *Invite students to help you write a few lines of your weekend journal entry.*

OR

✐ *Encourage a volunteer to write in front of the class.* Have the rest of the class assist by adding words and sentences. (If the student is a reluctant writer or English language learner you may want to serve as scribe as the student dictates.)

✐ *Assess student progress.* How did students do during discussions? Are they ready to write? Do you need to call up a small group and guide them while they write their entries?

Guided Writing

- *Implement guided writing during a whole-class lesson.*
  - Meet with table groups. Rotate to tables as students work on their individual pieces. Have each student at the table read his or her piece aloud. Ask the other group members to pay compliments and offer suggestions.
  - Invite a student volunteer in each table group to read her or his piece and tell what else she or he is going to write. Have the other team members write a suggested next line or word the writer could use. (The suggestions might be written on a sticky note or sentence strip to give to the writer.)

- *Implement guided writing with a temporary specific-needs group.* Meet with a different group every Monday (or Tuesday). (Most teachers use weekend webs and journals only once a week.)

- *Implement guided writing with an intervention group.* Group the struggling writers who need extra help and meet with them briefly to help them get started at the beginning of the session or to review their work at the end of the session. You might invite one or two of the class' stronger writers to serve as models and may need to show more examples. These students may need to illustrate their entries before writing.

- *Assess student progress.* Can students now work independently or do they need to continue to meet in a group to finish their work?

Independent Writing

- *Remind students to refer to the rubric for the skill or strategy, your model, and any shared writing pieces for guidance.*

- *Circulate through the room while the students write.* Prompt and support individual students as needed.

- *Offer a three-ring circus* (Pat Cunningham's term). Let students choose how they want to work:
  1. in a group with you
  2. in pairs, talking about their writing as they go
  3. independently at their desk

- *Assess student progress.* Do students apply what they have learned from the modeled and shared writing lessons in their own writing? Do they need to return to a guided group format?

Guided Conferring

- *Have students read their work to each other in small groups,* using the rubric as a guideline for compliments and suggestions. (Weekend webs and journal entries are a fluency tool, and it is best to not mark or grade them.)

Figure 4.10

Possible Weekend Web Minilessons Focusing on the Six Traits

 ### Ideas

- Model how to select ideas to develop in detail. Allow verbal sharing in pairs before students move on to write pieces.

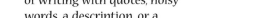 ### Word Choice

Model how to:

- Use interesting verbs, adjectives, nouns.

- Use metaphors, similes, and personification.

- Use "noisy words."

Organization

- There are different types of writing one might choose for weekend web topics:
  - letter
  - story
  - recipe
  - how-to-piece
  - description
  - poem

- Model inner organization:
  - beginning and ending a piece of writing with quotes, noisy words, a description, or a feeling
  - developing ideas in chronological order
  - setting up and solving a problem.

 ### Sentence Fluency

- Watch out for sentences that all begin the same.

- Watch out for sentences that are all long or all short.

 ### Voice

- Show how voice can be developed in a weekend web using:
  - humor
  - dialogue
  - emotions
  - one's unique opinion or reaction to an event

Conventions

- Reread your piece and add punctuation, capital letters, and correct spellings.

- Write freely at first and pay attention to conventions later.

- Weekend webs and journal entries are all about fluency; no red marks please!

✎ *Conduct "read-arounds."* Have students, at their tables or sitting in small circles, take turns reading their pieces. Ask the other students to offer compliments and suggestions. Rotate from group to group, guiding the process as necessary.

✎ *Conduct a hunt-and-share.* Choose one criterion in the rubric (including a sensory detail, for example). Ask students to find an example in their own work and the share it with a partner. Choose one child to share his or her example with the whole class. Select another teaching point for students to hunt for and share.

Discussion Questions

1. What are some of the problems with the weekend news routine? Do your students enjoy it? Are you able to use it successfully? Explain.

2. How do weekend webs compare with weekend news? What is similar/ different? What do you like about each? What are the advantages of weekend webs for your students? Explain. How do weekend webs help intermediate students write personal narratives?

3. What does it mean to write only what you can fit into a one-inch frame? How is this kind of short, focused writing helpful to students? How long should weekend journal entries be?

4. Create a weekend web and journal entry you might use as a model. Select a topic to web, and write a paragraph or two about it. How does doing this make you feel?

5. What are some of the skills/strategies/traits you might teach and reinforce using weekend webs and journal entries? Explain. How would you use a weekend web/journal entry to teach new skills or to reinforce ones you've already taught?

6. How can you support your students with guided writing when they write their weekend webs and journal entries? Which option appeals to you most?

Try It in Your Classroom

✎ Try a weekend web/journal entry with your class next Monday. Plan what your modeled web will look like and what you will include from your weekend. Select a small, everyday event to write about instead of an outing. Does this influence your students to select a small event from their web to write about?

✐ Look at ways to guide weekend web writing sessions, choose one, and try it with your class. What about it works for you? Will you need to pull students into guided groups every time?

✐ Think about why is it preferable not to mark up a child's weekend journal entry. Select five students per week to respond to, and write comments, positive and content-related only, on sticky notes applied to their journal entries. Stamp or put a star on the other entries to show you've read them. How does this improve the quality of their writing or motivation to write?

✐ Try different ways of allowing students to share their weekend journal entries: in pairs, at tables, and from the author's chair.

Chapter Five

Write This Way! Patterned Writing, Text Structure, and Author's Craft

Writing is a tool, an art, and a story.
—*Alex*

Some of us remember living through and surviving "predictable literature." Everyone read predictable, repetitive texts—books like *Brown Bear, Brown Bear, What Do You See?* by Bill Martin Jr.—to their students and then had the students write their own versions. Entire first grades wrote "White Ghost, White Ghost, What Do You See?" stories for Halloween. Some of my teacher friends had their students write new verses every month, all year long. They were bleary-eyed by January; by March they were sick to death of the pattern.

Writing patterns offer emerging writers or English language learners wonderful scaffolds for organizing their writing and ideas (Farnan and Dahl 2003). Over-reliance on patterns, however, makes students reluctant to write on their own. Students need a balance of writing opportunities to develop into skilled writers. Some problems you may have experienced with patterned writing include:

✎ Students have difficulty thinking of ideas and organization when asked to write on their own.

✎ Student writing becomes stilted and unsophisticated.

The lessons in this chapter are fresh spins on the concept of patterned writing that are sophisticated enough for students at any grade level. They work with both narrative and expository writing.

What Is Patterned Writing?

When we introduce our students to a variety of prose patterns and allow them to analyze these patterns, students are empowered to use the patterns in their own writing. The definition of "patterns" here is broadened to include story structure; repetition of events, dialogue, or lines; style; vocabulary; and even expository structure. In essence, a pattern is the way in which an author has organized his or her writing.

In her landmark book *Wondrous Words* (1999), Katie Wood Ray lays out the steps in studying an author's craft and organization: Why did this author write in this way? How does it help the message? What can we name it? (Give it a kid-friendly term students will remember.) How might we use this organization in our own writing?

We can use this way of studying author's craft to analyze any text for organizational patterns and then use those patterns to teach writing, helping students "write this way"—a method of mimicking and learning how authors organize their writing.

Benefits of Patterned Writing

Patterned writing has many benefits for students of all ages:

- It gives students tools they can use in their own writing.

- It gives students clear criteria for evaluating their writing.

- It works well in small-group guided writing lessons.

- It is especially helpful for emerging writers and English language learners.

Learning by Example

If you want to be a professional baseball player, you watch a game played by the pros. If you want to learn how to ballroom dance, you could do worse than watch one of those reality shows where professional dancers are paired with fading movie and television stars. If you want to be a writer, you study what authors do and emulate that in your own writing. Before I began to write professional books, I studied how some of my favorite teacher authors—Regie Routman, Linda Hoyt, Stephanie Harvey—write their books for teachers and tried to incorporate the elements that work for them into my unique style. Someday I plan to write a book or two for children. You can bet I will analyze the stories of my favorite children's authors before I begin.

Likewise, we must help our students read like writers and pick up pointers from the writing pros, authors of both fiction and nonfiction. It's important to capture your analysis of text organization and style in some tangible way. Katie Wood Ray's chart (see Figure 5.1) is one of the most valuable teaching tools I have; I use it with students of all ages. Usually I create it on chart paper, so students can refer to it during writing workshop, and flip through a pad full of these charts all year long to decide how to organize their texts. I also return to these anchor lessons often during whole-class lessons and guided writing in small groups.

Analyzing Fiction

Repetition as a Literary Device

Before reading *The Three Little Hawaiian Pigs and the Magic Shark* (1981), by Donivee Martin Laird, to a class of third graders, I ask them to watch out for words and events that repeat. When I finish, all hands go up:

The shark always says huff and puff.

The pigs then tell him "not by the hair of my chinny-chin-chin."

The pigs each build a house and then go and play.

The shark goes to each house and tries to blow it down.

Figure 5.1

Craft, Techniques, and Organization Analysis

What is the author doing?	Why is the author doing this?	What can I (we) call this crafting (or organizing) technique? Name it!	Have I (we) ever seen another author do this?	How can I (we) use this technique in my (our) own writing?

Adapted from Ray, 1999.

After also reading a version of *The Three Billy Goats Gruff*, we conclude that these authors probably told these stories around a fire in the "olden days" before television. The repetitive events and dialogue made the story longer and invited the listeners to chime in. I explain that we can use this pattern of three in our own writing, and we record this type of organization on a chart (see Figure 5.2).

Sometimes naming the technique takes a bit of prompting, but students are mostly better at this than adults. (One class I worked with named the repetition-in-threes technique "third time is a charm.") Students easily recall the techniques when they've named them as a class. Intermediate students might want to keep these charts in their writer's notebook so they can add other examples from their reading. And students are never too old to create stories based on the pattern of three. They might write about nagging their parents three times, at which point the parents finally relent. Or they could write about their repeated attempts to learn a new sport or hobby and incorporate repeated events and dialogue. The possibilities are endless, and your class will demonstrate great creativity in brainstorming their own list of writing possibilities.

When I created text innovations with small guided writing groups of second graders, I met with each group to brainstorm the words and events to be repeated in their story, which they entered on a story planning chart like the one in Figure 5.3. Before writing, each group then acted out their story for the class and the other students in the class paid compliments and made suggestions.

Figure 5.2

Repetition Analysis				
What is the author doing?	Why is the author doing this?	What can I (we) call this crafting (or organizing) technique? Name it!	Have I (we) ever seen another author do this?	How can I (we) use this technique in my (our) own writing?
In *The Three Hawaiian Pigs and the Magic Shark*, Donivee Laird repeats events: • The pigs each build a house. • The shark goes to their homes to blow them down. He also repeats words.	To make the story longer and more interesting, and to invite the listener to chime in	Three-Time Repeater	Many authors have done this in folk stories: • *The Three Bears* • *The Three Billy Goats Gruff*	We could write about . . . • begging our parents for something and finally getting it the third time • learning to do something and after three tries finally succeeding • a bad haircut/hair color and returning for a redo that keeps getting worse

Figure 5.3

Story Planning Chart: Third Time Is a Charm

Directions: Use this sheet to picture key events and write down key words as you plan your story. Maybe act it out to see if it makes sense.

Name: _____ Title of My Story: _____

Setting	Characters	Problem

Repeated Event 1	Repeated Event 2	Repeated Event 3
Repeated Words:	Repeated Words:	Repeated Words:

Solution to the Problem	Ending	

Adapted from Thompkins and McGee, 1989.

One group came up with a clever story about a soccer game. Three different players tried to kick a goal, missed, and tripped and fell. The repeated words were, "Oh, no, we didn't make our goal. Let's try again." Wanting a "third time is a charm" resolution, the group decided the smallest player would kick a goal and the goalie would trip while blocking it.

The students each chose a portion of text to write. While they worked, I conferred briefly with each one. We combined our papers, and I typed up the story. They each received a copy and together we edited and revised it by adding lines and rearranging portions of the text.

Beginnings/Endings

We've all read boring elementary school pieces that begin, "One day," or "Once upon a time," or "My name is," or "I am going to tell you about the time that." Text analysis is an excellent tool for helping students identify effective beginnings and endings that authors use to grab their readers.

A class of first graders (but you can teach this lesson at any grade level) sit patiently on the rug in front of me. I ask them each to grab a favorite picture book and sit on top of it while they wait for me to call on them to share their example. One by one they each stand by my rocking chair and read the beginning of their story aloud. This takes a good thirty minutes, and I am amazed that nobody is antsy yet. The magic of books has them spellbound. We record on a chart two techniques we've noticed so far that authors use to begin their stories—a "noisy" word or dialogue. When I ask the students if any of the books that they selected began, "One day," Timmy raises his hand and explains that maybe the students should stay away from that one. Everyone giggles at his telling remark.

I decide to provide a guided writing opportunity using the information we've charted. I explain that my daughter Rebecca and I had recently gone on a spring walk and heard a loud pecking noise coming from above. We looked up and spotted a woodpecker pounding away at a telephone pole. I ask the students, in table groups, to write a beginning for my story. I work my way around to each table and give them an overhead transparency and pen. (They love these cool tools!) I also ask probing questions and have them act out their suggested beginning. Later, each group stands next to the overhead projector to share their beginnings with the class. Here are three:

Tap, tap, tap. She was skerd as she crost the stret her hart was pownding and she rounded up the konr.
  —Rebecca, Natalie, and James

"What's that noise?" I asked as I was walking. "Rebecca, did you hear that noise," I said.
  —Richard and Danny

Tap, tap, tap, tap. Mrs. O., our reading teacher, heard a sound. She was wondering what it was. "Oh my God," she said to Rebecca. "I think it's coming from the wire!"
  —McClain, Caiseen, Alexander, and Danielle

In subsequent lessons I take the same guiding writing approach to endings. Each student shares the ending of their favorite picture book; we chart some of the main techniques authors use; then we try out one of the approaches in small guided writing groups and share it with the class.

Later students remember and refer to these anchor lessons and experiences as they create beginnings and endings for their own writing during writing workshop.

Analyzing Nonfiction

Organizational Structure

Mr. Clark dumps a big bag of nonfiction texts on the front table. The fourth grade students gasp at the messy mountain of books. He explains that he needs them to help him organize his books into categories. By doing this, they will learn how authors of nonfiction texts organize their texts.

He opens several texts and reads from them. Then the class decides how to label those texts, and Mr. Clark records the information on a copy of Katie Wood Ray's chart (see Figure 5.1). Eventually they include one example for each type of nonfiction text identified by Jan Dole (1997); see Figure 5.4.

Mr. Clark leaves the messy book pile in the room for several more days and calls students up in teams to read more of them, add them to the chart, and organize them in stacks. Throughout the year, as the class writes various kinds of nonfiction, they use the chart and these anchor texts (now neatly shelved) to help them. The students also continue to analyze and identify text structures wherever they find them: in social studies and science texts and articles and other nonfiction (see Figure 5.5).

A Nonfiction Writer's Club

Writing workshop is an ideal place to incorporate patterned writing and text analysis, since some young writers naturally begin to write nonfiction. By October, Miss Thrane had a group of first grade students, mostly boys, who were attempting to write non-fiction on their own, usually mixing off-the-top-of-their-heads facts with opinions and "I likes." McClain began one of his pieces this way: *inthlastsen vocns yoos to urupt*

Figure 5.4

Categories of Nonfiction Texts	
Type of Text	Cue Words or Elements
Cause and Effect	since, so, due to, because, reasons why or if
Problem/Solution	problem, one reason that, this is caused by
Question/Answer	how, when, where, what, why, who
Sequence	first, next, then, finally, until, before, after
Compare/Contrast	likewise, different, same as, on the other hand
Explanation	characteristics, features, parts, subtopics
Description	more fictionlike: sensory words, emotions, thoughts

Adapted from Dole, 1995.

Figure 5.5

Nonfiction Structure Analysis				
What is the author doing?	Why is the author doing this?	What can I (we) call this crafting (or organizing) technique? Name it!	Have I (we) ever seen another author do this?	How can I (we) use this technique in my (our) own writing?
The Living Rainforest, by Nic Bishop (2000); tells about the rainforest.	To explain the various categories of rainforest information	Describer/Teller	Many times. Our social studies and science books are mostly like this.	When we write our mission reports, we will write them like this.
Kids Rule, by Kimberly Weinberger (2000); lists problems that kids have solved.	To teach us about problems and solutions that young people have worked on	Problem/Solution Yikes/Fix it!	Yes, the teacher read aloud to us from *A River Ran Wild*, by Lynne Cherry (1992). People cleaned up a polluted river.	We could research what good things students in our community are doing and write about that.

[In the last century volcanoes used to erupt]. His message is sophisticated, even though he is an emerging reader and writer. He really wants to write nonfiction.

Instead of conducting a minilesson on nonfiction writing with the entire class, I often invite a small group of students to work with me in a "nonfiction club." During writing workshop I call them over to my table and we analyze some nonfiction texts. Next I guide the group as we write about a topic they have selected. Each student writes a fact on a sentence strip (a cool tool) and adds it to our "report" in the pocket chart. Together we also write a beginning and an ending. Over the next week I convene similar voluntary nonfiction clubs for students who wish to learn some nonfiction writing tips such as creating a table of contents or incorporating headings and captions. Eventually, I set up a center containing nonfiction books students can borrow and students' nonfiction writing they can read. The nonfiction club becomes a popular place!

Guided writing lessons are easy with patterned books. The strong models we provide from published literature and nonfiction texts support each step of the scaffold. The criteria we use to build our assessment rubrics also grow out of our experiences analyzing what authors do to organize and build their craft. For example, when students analyze a text and discover repeating events and words, their rubric for their own writing includes those elements as well.

Scaffolded lesson

A Patterned Writing Lesson in Action

Identifying Examples

As I read *My Mama Had a Dancing Heart*, by Libba Moore Gray (1995), aloud to a class of fourth graders for the second time, I give them a new purpose for listening. We are going to create a text analysis chart and need to name the organizational technique this author uses.

Jason raises his hand. "It looks like the author is repeating the seasons. Can we call this book a 'seasonal repeater'?" I ask each table to discuss the new term, and Jason's idea wins hands down. This heartwarming book is about a mother and daughter's relationship and how they spend time together through the seasons. For each season the book includes a dance (the flower-opening-hello spring ballet, the dolphin-arching-hello summer ballet). They also savor a special food or treat (hot spiced tea, lemonade) and share in a unique activity (piling seashells, making snow angels).

Gray also enjoys playing with words (*plash-splashing* and *seashell-pile*). I ask the students to come up with a name for this special language pattern, which appears on every page. Someone suggests we call these interesting words "two pairs," and all hands rise in favor of that clever title. As we reread the book, we add "seasonal repeater" and "two pairs" to the chart (see Figure 5.6).

"I noticed that the book begins and ends with the same lines," Haley volunteers. I am relieved that someone noticed this without my pointing it out. I reread the repeating beginning and ending aloud: *"My mama had a dancing heart and she shared that heart with me."* We add this technique to the chart. The students name it a "story sandwich," because the beginning and ending match like the bread on a sandwich. Clever!

Figure 5.6

Structure in *My Mama Had a Dancing Heart*, by Libba Moore Gray				
What is the author doing?	Why is the author doing this?	What can I (we) call this crafting (or organizing) technique? Name it!	Have I (we) ever seen another author do this?	How can I (we) use this technique in my (our) own writing?
Repeating events through the seasons: • a dance • food, drink • activity	As a way to give a pattern or structure to the story	Seasonal Repeater	*The Little House*, by Virginia Lee Burton	We could write about: • a family member • a friend • a pet • our school
She uses pairs of related words: • frog-hopping • leaf-growing • plash-splashing	To sound nice To make the words more interesting and fun	Two Pairs		We can add these to any story or poem.
She begins and ends the book with the same line.	To come full circle and make it complete	Story Sandwich		We can use the same line for a beginning and ending.

Modeling

"Class, I am going to copy the pattern Libba Gray has used in this book and write a piece about spending precious time with my grandmother as a child." I draw a web on a projected transparency and brainstorm an activity, food, and two–pair word for each season. I also tell the class I will use the "sandwich" technique for the beginning and ending of my piece. I write about one season in front of the class:

> My grandmother was the playful kind. She never passed up the chance to have fun with me!
>
> Every spring when the blossoms-pink come peek-peeking out, we'd dig in her lovely garden green. After a mud-squishing time, we'd sip Pepsi and sit munch-munching graham crackers brown.

Guided Writing

After my demonstration, the students turn to partners and check my sample for elements from the chart. They conclude that I am on my way. As a class we decide they'll practice these techniques using the topic of our school through the seasons. I assign one season to each table. The groups write their brainstorming webs on large pieces of construction paper and include "two pairs" terms. I rotate to each group to check their ideas before they write. I also guide each group through some of the composing process. I ask each student to jot down the next line for their group on a sticky note. We discuss their ideas, and they continue writing as I move on to the next group. Finally each group projects a transparency containing their work and shares it with the class. Here's group one's effort:

> ### Our School in Summer
>
> The hot blazing sun comes out and clouds run away. The school is empty except for the chit-chattering bike-riding kids. But mind-rotting kids are stuck at home without school.

Independent Writing/Small Guided Groups

During the guided group writing, I notice that students are having difficulty sticking to the patterns used in the book. To prepare them to write independently, I have them fill in a prewriting graphic organizer that includes the elements for each season. They can check it for guidance while writing and while conferring with me and their classmates. (A grid like this is simple to create and can be used for any patterns you want students to mimic.)

Robbie's prewriting chart is shown in Figure 5.7.

Guided Conferring/Class Book

I call small groups of writers to my back table for conferences. Students read at least a section or two of their piece aloud. The other group members pay compliments and make suggestions based on the criteria on the prewriting-chart-turned-rubric. Many of the students have repeated the word *eat* or *drink* in their piece. During

Figure 5.7

Robbie's Prewriting Chart

My Topic: My Cat, Mocha

My Beginning/Ending Line: My cat, Mocha, is the fluffy kind and she's always by my side.

Include "two pairs" in your chart.

Describe the season	Fall	Winter	Spring	Summer
	Cold-crisp mornings	Thick white sheets of rain-wonderland	Sniff-smell Fresh spring air Yellow-orange flowers	Red-orange morning sun
What you do in the season	Open presents (birthdays)	Leave for Tahoe	Run, allergies	Throw Nerf balls, skip
What you eat or drink	Warm turkey sliced	Sip-sipping warm milk	Fish	Coffee cake

our guided conference they replace these words with words like *gobbled*, *munched*, *savored*, *enjoyed*, and *sipped*!

The students have written such beautifully organized pieces about parents, sports, hobbies, and pets, filled with their unique voices, that we compile them into a class book. Anthony's piece, about hamsters, his favorite creatures, makes me smile. I've known him since kindergarten and over the years he has written hamster reports, poems, and stories. Here is his entertaining fall section:

> My hamster has a funny face and he shares that face with me.
> In the fall my hamster gallop-scurries and leap-bounds over soft-fluffy grass under the hot warm sun like a tiny jumping jackrabbit. He sometimes crawls under the crunchy leaves. They occasionally fall on him and he thinks, "Aaahhh, I'm under attack!" My hamster chomps on seeds and gulps down water and V8 juice.

Jacob presented his, which is included below in its entirety, to his mother for Mother's Day!

> ### Mom Through the Months
> My mom and I have a lot of fun during all the seasons.
> On a flower-picking, bird-chirping lively spring day we smell flowers.
> When Easter comes we'll gobble up chocolate Easter eggs.
> On a fire-blazing, b.b.q.-burning warm summer day it will be my birthday.
> I'll open presents and we'll scarf down chocolate cake.
> On a multicolored leaf-falling, pumpkin-carving, tree-climbing autumn day

we'll jump in leaves and devour Halloween candy, pie, and turkey.
On a snowflake-falling, snowball-throwing, snowman-building, cold winter day
we'll go to Garden Grove to visit my family and sip hot chocolate.
My mom and I have fun during all the seasons.

SCAFFOLDED Patterned Writing/Text Structure Lessons

Scaffolded lesson

Patterned writing lessons work well with either fiction or nonfiction. You can analyze fictional texts for beginnings, endings, plot development, and word choice. When analyzing nonfiction texts, study the organization of the text, word choice, development of details and ideas, and sentence fluency.

Objectives

- Students identify organizational patterns or elements of craft in one or more texts.

- Students create a rubric that lists elements of the pattern or skill.

- Students, in small groups, produce guided writing that includes the pattern or skill.

- Students write their own pieces using the pattern or skill.

- Student writing has more voice and is better organized.

Identifying Examples

- *Ask students to help you analyze a text for organizational patterns or author's craft.* For fiction you might concentrate on the plot or story structure. With non-fiction, help students identify the category (see Figure 5.4).

- *Begin a class chart (see Figure 5.1) capturing the results of your analysis.* Discuss the text organization from the author's perspective. What is the author doing? Why? How does this fit the text and help the reader?

- *Introduce cool tools.* Bring in a pile of books and allow students to sort them according to category and method of organization. Use sticky notes to mark the teaching points such as interesting beginnings or endings.

- *Assess student progress.* Do the students need more examples of this kind of text from either student samples or other books? Can they verbalize their observations?

Modeling

- *Brainstorm using the class-created chart.* Write on the whiteboard, chart paper, or a projected transparency. Think aloud to point out that you are incorporating the criteria the class identified on the chart. Have students turn to a partner and discuss your writing.

Write your patterned piece. Reiterate the skill you are focusing on: *I'm going to try to organize my piece using the compare-and-contrast elements we captured on our chart.* Think aloud as you go. Use a web or other graphic organizer (story map, Venn diagram, etc.; see Figures 2.1 and 5.8). Talk as you write each sentence. Pretend to get stuck. Scratch words out and rewrite. Go back to the text you analyzed and show how you are adapting the organizational method or skill to your writing.

Reread your writing. Tell students that good writers reread as they revise and think of what to write next.

Check your writing against the rubric or chart and add to it. Have you included the points listed in the chart? Ask students to tell what they think is important or what they liked about your writing and add their ideas to the chart.

Introduce cool tools. Stop and check student understanding using thumbs-up or thumbs-down signals. "Does this word sound right here? Read it with me. Do you like this?"

Assess student progress. Are students ready to write on their own? Are they in the "mood" to write? Do they need a shared writing step, or can you jump to independent writing?

Shared Writing

Invite students to help you write a fiction or nonfiction piece. Have students make suggestions orally or write their ideas on sticky notes or a slate. Discuss these ideas and use some of them in a few sentences of shared writing.

OR

Encourage a volunteer to write in front of the class. If the student is a reluctant writer or English language learner, you may want to write as the student dictates.

Assess student progress. How did students do during the discussions? Are they ready to write? Do you need to call up a small group and guide them while they write individually?

Guided Writing

Implement guided writing during a whole-class lesson. Meet with table groups as they work on group patterned pieces. Remind them to refer to the chart and the example text they analyzed. Encourage students to stick to the pattern but to add their own voice and ideas.

Form a nonfiction club during writing workshop. Invite interested students to meet with you to study structure in nonfiction. Have student select a structure to use as a pattern for their own writing. Confer with individual students.

Implement guided writing during guided reading. After a guided reading group has read a fiction or nonfiction text, lead them in analyzing its structure. Make a

Figure 5.8

Brainstorming/Organizing My Patterned Writing

Name: _____ Date: _____

The text(s) I am patterning my writing after is (are): _____

Pattern from the text	How I will use the pattern in my writing

Figure 5.9

Possible Minilessons for Patterned Writing Focusing on the Six Traits

 ### Ideas

- Read about authors. Where do they get their ideas? How does being a reader help you write?

- Keep a running class list of ideas "borrowed" from authors.

- Ask students to keep track of ways authors build details.

 ### Word Choice

- Find and list words commonly used in mysteries, love stories, picture books, etc.

- Find and list words associated with each category of nonfiction (see Figure 5.4).

- Hunt for key transition words and make a chart.

Organization

- Examine various types of fiction and nonfiction picture books and discuss the different patterns. Allow students to form interest groups to learn to write nonfiction stories in the various forms.

- Have students rewrite a piece in a different genre. Model using the same information to turn a story into a letter, a report into a poem, a report into an advertisement.

 ### Sentence Fluency

- Reproduce a page or two of text and give each student a copy. Have students, using highlighters, mark longer and shorter sentences. Discuss how authors vary sentence length. (With primary students, use an actual big book and highlighter tape or Wikki sticks in two colors.)

- What are some ways authors make their sentences more interesting? Hunt with your class for examples and chart them.

 ### Voice

- What makes a text unique or funny?

- How does the way a text is organized make it formal or informal?

Conventions

- Are conventions the same or different in fiction and nonfiction? Compare and contrast.

- Use Katie Wood Ray's chart to examine how authors use conventions (Angelillo 2002).

chart of what you find. Write a piece together, each student or pair of students working on a portion of the text. Have them write on index cards or other cool tools and then work out an effective order on a pocket chart. Working as a group, add transitions and a beginning and ending.

✐ *Assess student progress.* Can students now work independently or do they need to continue to work in a group? Does their writing incorporate the organizational method or writing skill of the text they analyzed?

Independent Writing

✐ *Give students a copy of the chart to use as a checklist as they write.* Older students can copy the chart into their writer's notebook. Students can prewrite on organizers (see Figures 5.8 and 5.9).

✐ *Confer with individual students as needed.*

✐ *Assess student progress.* Do students apply what they have learned from the modeled and shared writing lessons in their own writing? Collect and analyze student writing. Do they need to return to a guided group format?

Guided Small-Group Conferring

✐ *Have students read their work to one another in small groups,* using the rubric as a guideline for compliments and suggestions.

OR

✐ *Lead a group conference.* Invite one small group to meet with you. Conduct a roundtable discussion using these prompts: *Read your best line. Read your best word. Check your piece against each item on the chart. How you are using the pattern? What is giving you trouble?* Encourage students to turn and talk to a partner to make the discussion go faster. Select a student from the group and lead the group members in helping that student improve his or her work.

OR

✐ *Lead group table conferences.* Ask the students to read their pieces at their tables and have their tablemates respond with compliments, then give suggestions for improving the piece using the rubric or chart. Have each table vote on which piece followed the pattern best and read that piece aloud to the whole class. Why does this piece follow the pattern? Be specific.

Discussion Questions

1. When someone mentions patterned writing, what do you think of? How have you used patterned writing in the past? Explain what worked for you. How does analyzing text structure help students at all grade levels in their writing?

2. What do you like about Katie Wood Ray's chart? What are some ways you might incorporate it into whole-class or small-group lessons? How will you display and store completed charts so students may refer to them as they write?

3. Why is letting students name the technique being studied so powerful? Do they remember the lesson more easily? Is naming a technique or strategy difficult for your students? How can you support students as they name elements of the author's craft or specific writing skills?

4. Why is studying how authors begin and end their texts helpful to young writers? Why is modeled and guided writing helpful in teaching students to write effective beginnings and endings?

5. Discuss the various types of structure used in nonfiction. In your own reading, notice how nonfiction authors use structure to convey their message. See if you can find examples of each nonfiction category over the course of a week. Is it helpful as a reader and writer to know about these structures?

Try It in Your Classroom

✐ Make a chart like the one in Figure 5.1. Use it in connection with a piece of fiction that repeats, like *The Three Bears*. Have older students read these stories to buddies in earlier grades.

✐ Use the chart with nonfiction books written by Gail Gibbons, Seymour Simon, or another author who is good at using description. What do the students notice about the organization and style of this work? Have your students write short picture books mimicking the style of this author.

✐ Analyze the organization of a chapter in a social studies or science text. Is it always the same or does it vary? Discuss findings with your colleagues and/or your students.

Chapter Six

Read and Write All About It! Expository Writing

I am inspired to work on a subject I enjoy. A report is successful when the reader develops knowledge about the subject and continues to give it thought.
—Jason

Whether you teach the popular second- or third-grade "animal" report or the dreaded fifth-grade "state" report, you know how much work it is to teach expository writing. Primary students generally start off being excited about the idea of lugging around a stack of nonfiction books for their research. They brag at home about finally getting to write a report just like the big kids. Something happens along the way though, and by fifth or maybe even fourth grade just the mention of the word *report* causes parents, students, and teachers to feel exhausted before the work even begins.

What is so daunting about expository writing? Think about all the important skills that go into it. Students need to read and synthesize information from a number of sources. Then they take notes in their own words, infer main ideas that make sense, and write paragraphs and topic sentences to support their points. No wonder everyone grimaces at the thought of writing reports. It's hard work!

Whether you are a veteran teacher who's been teaching report writing for years or a brand-new teacher, the ideas in this chapter are designed to strengthen your students' report writing skills. Guided expository writing supports students' learning, helps them internalize that learning, and makes the whole process more enjoyable. Specifically, students:

- receive additional modeling and guided practice before writing on their own

- practice the "pieces" of report writing step-by-step in a supported atmosphere

- internalize report writing skills as they work in cooperative teams and verbalize their concerns and understanding

- learn to recognize good report writing skills as they score their group report and other groups' reports.

The Guided Writing Approach to Expository Text

Students encounter many problems and difficulties as they write reports:

- identifying main ideas in the research materials

✐ taking notes in their own words rather than copying their sources verbatim

✐ writing opening paragraphs, topic sentences, thesis statements, and closing paragraphs.

It's no wonder many students don't know where to begin!

Guided report writing, like other guided writing lessons, supports students with an intermediate collaborative step before students write independently. Students write reports or portions of reports in cooperative groups that you guide. You may lead all the groups simultaneously, visiting each one in turn, or convene groups one at a time over the course of several days. Another option is to meet with a small group of struggling writers to help them practice composing reports together.

It helps to break down the task of report writing and teach a series of minilessons over a few weeks before your students write their reports. Each skill, from composing a topic sentence to writing a strong conclusion, can require any combination of scaffolding steps, including identifying examples in texts, modeling, whole-class shared writing, cooperative guided groups, and independent writing.

Whatever the particular skill, you can either show students examples from expository text to make your teaching points or, better, allow students to hunt for their own examples and then draw conclusions. Look at how Margie Musante allows her fifth graders to study and identify how authors of expository text begin their pieces (the same approach could be used for endings): "Today we are going to learn how nonfiction writers write beginnings." She passes out a variety of nonfiction texts, and students, in teams, hunt for examples of beginning lines and paragraphs. As the students read these beginnings aloud, Mrs. Musante creates a large chart of their findings, then goes a step further and asks students to name the categories of beginnings. Here's what they come up with (see Figure 6.1):

✐ quotes

✐ questions

✐ big problem/action

✐ little-known fact or statistic

✐ memory flashback

✐ thoughts and feelings

To help your students practice identifying examples of these beginnings, simply number the types from 1 through 6. Then, as you read examples from books and

Figure 6.1

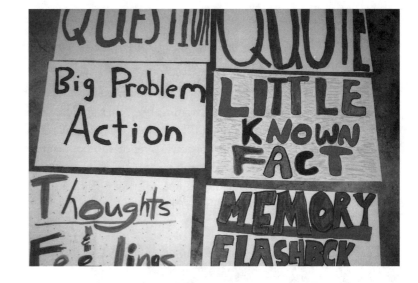

other nonfiction texts, ask your students to identify which type of beginning it is by holding up the corresponding number of fingers. You may also invite students to take turns giving examples to the class. Figures 6.2 and 6.3 are guides to good beginnings and endings in expository text.

When I worked in Robyn Arthur's fifth grade, we taught students that a good opening paragraph of an expository five-paragraph essay has a catchy beginning, a thesis statement, and a "sneak preview" or "commercial" of what the three middle paragraphs will be about. Unfortunately, expository authors don't always follow this formula to the letter, so I wrote an example myself (see Figure 6.4) and made copies for each pair of students. Then I asked them to underline the catchy beginning sentence in green, the thesis statement in yellow, and the preview of main topics in red. (You may also use actual text. Make a copy of a page or two from a book, or use an article in a children's weekly magazine if your students receive one.)

Using Everyday Examples

One especially effective but rather innovative way to support students is to use everyday examples. I often model writing a five-paragraph essay about my younger daughter's staying home from school. Students always perk up when I do; they love hearing about this kind of thing. Here's the essay:

> (*Introductory paragraph—Catchy beginning:*) Rebecca tiptoed into my bedroom early in the morning and whined, "Mommy, I don't feel so good." I noticed her droopy eyelids and felt her steaming hot forehead and I knew at once she was ill. (*Thesis statement:*) While she stayed home from school to recover, we had lots of fun together. (*Preview:*) We planned Bryan's birthday celebration, dug out old toys, and read a zillion books.
>
> (*Paragraph 1—Planned celebration:*) Rebecca and I made a list of the kinds of food we would make for her brother's birthday. We included all Bryan's favorites: pizza, salad, and chocolate cake. Also, we decided we'd all watch Star Wars movies at home and eat popcorn.

> (*Paragraph 2—Cleaned out old toys:*) After we planned Bryan's party, Rebecca laid on her bed sipping juice and resting while I held up old toys and dolls for her to consider giving away. Although she hated to part with some of them, she admitted her room is too cluttered with toys she's outgrown. We filled two big boxes to give away to charity.
> (*Paragraph 3—Read a zillion books:*) Rebecca began to get sleepy, so I sat on the edge of her bed and read to her for at least an hour. We laughed and even cried through some of her favorite stories from author Rosemary Wells. She chose a huge stack of picture books and we read almost all of them. Eventually, she dozed off.
> (*Ending paragraph—Catchy beginning sentence:*) At around 3 p.m. the fever seemed to lift and Rebecca exclaimed, "I'm feeling better now." (*Restatement of thesis:*) Even though she was sick today, we had fun together. (*Review:*) We accomplished a lot by planning Bryan's party, cleaning out her toys, and reading together. I'll miss her tomorrow when she is back at school!

If I'm short on time, I model writing the first and last paragraphs and just tell the students what the middle paragraphs contain.

Using Commercials

Another fun way to practice expository writing is with commercials. For example, you might ask students to help you write about a certain type of candy. You need to come up with a catchy general statement ("Yummies are the healthiest candy that delights your tongue") and a three-pronged sneak preview ("Yummies contain vitamins and minerals, are eaten by famous athletes the world over, and cost very little"). Practicing the building blocks of report writing by touting easy, high-interest products like this (or pizza, or cereal) helps students internalize how to write about more serious topics.

GUIDED Report-Writing Minilessons in Action

affolded lesson

Here are two minilessons that are easy to implement at any grade level; the basic steps can be used with any writing skill you wish to teach.

Writing Great Beginnings

- After identifying great catchy first sentences in expository texts and modeling how to write the various kinds, pass out overhead transparencies and ask students to write sample first sentences for a topic. Assign a type to each group or let them choose.

- Circulate to each group and guide their efforts.

- Have each group project the transparency containing their catchy sentence, and ask the other students to comment and respond.

- *Optional*: Have each student on a team create a different type of beginning sentence (quote, description, fact, question, etc.) on a different-color index

Figure 6.2

Guide to Catchy Report Beginnings	
Quote	"My lifelong dream was to find this ship," says Robert Ballard, the scientist who found the *Titanic*.
Description • of setting, character, event • flashback • reads like fiction	Hundreds of passengers excitedly waved good-bye for the very last time as the *Titanic* took off on her maiden voyage. The sun glistened on the water as the newly constructed vessel set sail to make history.
Fact • important statistic/fact • little-known or interesting fact	Little did the passengers of the *Titanic* know as they set sail that 1,500 of them would lose their lives on the famous ship.
Opinion	The *Titanic* is my favorite sunken ship to study because it was so elegant and strong and was filled with rich and famous people.
Question • single question • a series of questions	What is one of the most famous sunken ships of all time? Why did the *Titanic* disaster happen? What could have prevented the most famous sunken ship of all time from going down? Why didn't the crew see the iceberg that caused the fate of the ship?
Dialogue	"What is the most famous sunken ship of all time?" asked the teacher. "The *Titanic*!" shouted the students in unison. "I know why it is so famous," Danya volunteered.
Problem	The *Titanic* sank in 1912. Many explorers tried unsuccessfully to find the sunken treasure. Why did it take until 1985 to discover the famous luxury ship? What problems did explorers searching for it experience?

Adapted from Mariconda 2001 and Fletcher 2001.

card or strip. Then ask all the group members to glue their sample catchy sentences onto butcher paper and label them. They can display their posters or leave them on tables and take a "gallery tour" (see Appendix B).

Writing an Introductory Paragraph

✐ Ask students to work in teams of three to write about basketball.

✐ Ask students to restate what a beginning paragraph should contain (see Figure 2.4).

✐ List these elements on the board:
   1. catchy beginning sentence
   2. thesis statement summarizing what the essay is about

Figure 6.3

Guide to Great Report Endings	
Questions(s)	Wouldn't it be exciting to go on an expedition and see the site of the sunken *Titanic*? What kinds of other treasures and artifacts remain that need to be resurrected and brought to the surface? In time what other treasures will tell the story of the ill-fated ship?
Simple Wrap-up • return to beginning and say in a different way	As you can see, the *Titanic* holds an important place in history as the most famous sunken treasure of all time.
Create a Scene	Imagine the terror of the *Titanic* passengers who were left on the ship as it sank: the creaking wood, violins playing, the cold night air.
Warning or Call to Action	Since the awful *Titanic* disaster, shipbuilders have crafted instruments that help alert modern ships to danger more quickly. Still, the possibility of sinking remains a threat for every vessel. Scientists continue to search for safer means of navigation so the *Titanic* mishap will never be repeated.
Quotation	"The *Titanic's* sheer size, elegance, and publicity brought great importance to its sinking," says a noted documentary film producer.

Adapted from Mariconda 2001 and Fletcher 2001.

Figure 6.4

Example of an Opening Paragraph

What is one of the most famous sunken ships of all time? The *Titanic* is the sunken ship that many people agree is most well-known. The *Titanic* went down in history because of its size, its elegance, and its horrible fate.

3. sneak preview listing three topics that will be covered in detail in the paragraphs

- Assign the paragraph topics of teamwork, healthy exercise, and fun.
- Assign students to write sentence 1, 2, or 3.
- Move from group to group asking probing questions:
  - *Which catchy beginning sentence did you choose? Could you have selected another?*
  - *Does your thesis statement tell what the report will be about? Is it general enough?*
  - *Does your preview include all the points you will discuss in later paragraphs?*

✐ Have students combine and revise their sentences.

✐ Let each group share their example paragraph. They might use an overhead transparency or a large piece of construction paper. Here's an example of a possible opening paragraph:

(*Catchy first sentence*:) You don't have to be a famous former NBA player like Michael Jordan or Magic Johnson to love basketball. (*Thesis statement*:) Basketball is a great sport for kids of all ages. (*Sneak preview list*:) Basketball promotes teamwork, healthy exercise, and enjoyment.

Teaching the Five-Paragraph Essay

"What do you know about sunken ships and treasure?" I ask a class of fifth graders. After a quick partner share, many hands wave frantically. The very first student I call on tells about the Titanic, and other hands slide down with a sigh of disappointment or a whispered, "She took my answer." "Okay," I say, "many of you have read about the *Titanic* or seen the movie. We are going to read Gail Gibbons' book *Sunken Treasure* [1988] to learn more about the *Titanic* and other sunken ships. After we're finished, we will, in teams, write a report on the book, in order to learn valuable skills you'll need when you write reports on your own."

Over the next two and a half weeks, I present minilessons on each aspect of expository writing:

✐ how to write a five-paragraph essay: overview

✐ how to plan your main points based on your research

✐ how to take notes

✐ how to write an opening paragraph:
   ✐ catchy opening sentence
   ✐ thesis statement
   ✐ sneak preview of topics

✐ how to write a topic sentence

✐ how to write a paragraph

✐ how to write an ending

Each lesson follows the scaffolded steps. The first fifteen minutes are spent on identifying examples, modeling, and table group guided writing. During the remainder of each period, assigned heterogeneous teams work on their essay on sunken ships and treasure while I work with the struggling writers on the same assignments. (See Figure 6.5.)

Reading/Research

The first few days I present lessons in effective reading. We study the book's illustrations and headings, and each guided writing team group writes four things they wonder about the topic:

Figure 6.5

Daily Schedule for Guided Writing Lessons on Report Writing

✐ *Identifying examples in texts* (3 minutes).

✐ *Modeling/shared writing* (5 to 10 minutes). Either write an example yourself or ask students to help you in shared writing.

✐ *Guided writing at tables* (5 to 10 minutes). Choose an everyday topic or other high interest nonfiction topic. Have students, at their tables, write an example on a transparency and share it with the rest of the class.

✐ *Guided writing in assigned teams* (15 to 20 minutes). Have teams apply the skill practiced during the minilesson to their group report. (Work with special-needs students as necessary.)

✐ *I wonder how divers searched for ships before they had scuba gear.*

✐ *I wonder what equipment helps the divers locate and study the treasures they find.*

✐ *I wonder why and how they mark the grid on the ocean floor.*

✐ *I wonder how they preserve the treasures on the surface.*

They write these "wonderments" on sticky notes and group them into three or four categories, which become the main points of their report. Group Four's categories are:

✐ *We wonder how scientists study how the ships sink.*

✐ *We wonder how they search for the ships.*

✐ *We wonder what special equipment they use to find the ships.*

The students then read the book independently or with a partner. Each team assigns a recorder to takes notes on a piece of large construction paper, or each student writes on sticky notes and attaches them to the group chart. I leave my intervention group to work by themselves for a few minutes and make my way to each group, guiding them to reword the text rather than copy it verbatim. Jason says he has boiled down two pages of text to just two sentences. Hanna admits she is stuck and doesn't know how to reword what the text says. I ask her to tell me three key words, and together we come up with synonyms. She smiles and quickly jots down her ideas on a sticky note to contribute to her team's chart.

Guided Writing Teams

The guided writing team schedule is shown in Figure 6.6. Each group uses five large pieces of construction paper to write their group reports; one for the introduction, one each for the three middle paragraphs, and one for a conclusion. They hook their pages together with yarn, and I hang them in the hallway to read and evaluate (see Figure 6.7).

Figure 6.6

> ### Guided Writing Team Schedule (15 to 20 minutes per lesson)
>
> **Day 1:** Categorize your "wonderments" into three main points.
>
> **Day 2:** Share notes you've taken about these categories.
>
> **Day 3:** Write an introduction that includes a catchy first sentence, a thesis statement, and a sneak preview. Use sentence strips to write your individual contributions to the group piece. Rewrite your sentences with the help of the other group members if necessary and glue them on a large sheet of construction paper.
>
> **Days 6 to 9:** Write the middle three paragraphs. (Each pair can take one paragraph.)
>
> **Day 10:** Write the conclusion.
>
> **Day 11:** Recopy any messy text. Reread the report checking for errors.

Figure 6.7

The Intervention Group

Each day when we break into groups I work with the struggling writers—students who either just sit when it is time to write or simply refuse to participate. I don't believe in segregating this group of students for everything, but doing so for occasional writing assignments ensures that they internalize what I am teaching. (Figure 6.8 presents one approach to working with an intervention group; Figure 6.9 shows the result of combining students' writing into one piece.)

When we write paragraphs in this group, I am the scribe as we compose a topic sentence together. Then I pass out sentence strips, and pairs of students write details for the paragraph. We reread our writing chorally to confirm or reject our new ideas. One day when we reread, Arty realizes that the word *treasure* appears too often. The students suggest some synonyms. Antonio gloms on to the word *trinkets*, which we decide might not be exactly right. Arty dashed off for a thesaurus. I am thrilled to see these reluctant writers with such a "can-do" attitude and so engaged.

Figure 6.8

Expository Writing with an Intervention Group

cool tools

- *Select a cool tool*: index cards, sticky notes, sentence strips, large pieces of chart paper, small pieces of chart paper that can be hooked together with brads, yarn, or rings.

- *Take dictation*: As students dictate their ideas, guide their work and write it down.

- *Reread chorally*: Constantly reread the writing chorally as a group.

- *Ask every student to write*: Break a portion of the writing into small segments. Have each student write a sentence or two on her or his own to contribute to the group composition.

- *Combine students' writing*: Work with the group to combine all students' writing into one piece. Read it aloud together.

Figure 6.9

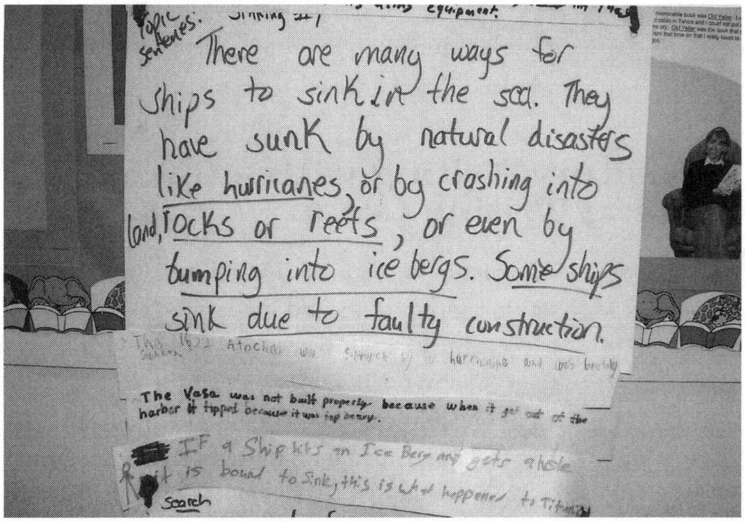

Hallway Scoring

All six of the group reports hang neatly in the hallway for all to see. The proud writing teams gather on the rug to help me decide how to evaluate our work. We discuss the elements of reports and create a quick rubric for the assignment. (Appendix D contains a sample rubric for expository text.) Over several days I choose groups to go out into the hallway and use the scoring rubric (see Figure 6.14). Students read every group's report and check off whether it includes the particular element or not. I am pleasantly surprised at just how seriously these young evaluators take their job. With poker faces, pencils in hand, they give each of the other teams a quick score (Figure 6.10). I'm not as concerned with numerical scores as with the quality of discussion and thinking that occurs during this evaluation. One of the struggling writers finds several detail sentences in other groups' reports that don't seem to fit. Other students notice that some groups need a stronger

Figure 6.10

conclusion. After the scoring session, we discuss the top problems they spotted in the writing: not restating the thesis in the ending and including details that don't fit as main ideas. The groups decide to reexamine the examples we constructed in whole-class lessons and then revise their pieces.

Expository Writing with a Guided Reading/Writing Group

The picture in Figure 6.11 is from a series of lessons I taught to a guided reading/ writing group of second graders over a three-day period. We began by previewing a leveled text about sharks and asking what we wondered about these marine creatures (Figure 6.12). I allowed pairs of students to select the heading and section they would read in the text. They wrote their shark facts they learned on large sheets of construction paper and illustrated them (see Figure 6.13). I conferred with each pair of writers and as they revised and wrote final copies. As a group they dictated to me the introductory and concluding paragraphs. We hooked our report pieces together for display with yarn.

On the final day, we wrote a guided poem next to the shark report. First, the children each scanned the report for a word or phrase they liked or thought was important. Then we went around the circle; each child dictated his or her word or phrase while I wrote them down. The result was a quick guided poem that synthesized what we had learned:

Sharks

Carnivores catch by surprise
Cannibals
Timid creatures
Swimming 37 miles per hour
Timid, unique
Big fish
Camouflage

Figure 6.11

Figure 6.12

Figure 6.13

SCAFFOLDED **Guided Expository Writing Lessons**

These lessons work well with any type of expository text: reports, essays, descriptions. Try focusing on just one expository writing skill at a time, like writing a topic sentence or paragraph, and working through all the steps: identifying examples, modeling, shared writing, guided writing, independent writing, and guided conferring/evaluation.

Objectives

✐ Identify the organizational elements of excellent expository writing, including an interesting beginning, topic sentences, relevant details, and a strong ending.

✐ Model expository writing using everyday examples.

✐ In guided groups, write pieces of reports as well as one complete report.

⊘ Evaluate the reports in order to improve them.

⊘ Strengthen ideas and organization.

Identifying Examples

⊘ *Ask students to help you identify various components of expository writing in nonfiction books.* Categorize books according to overall organization. (See Chapter 5, Figure 5.4).

⊘ *Teach separate lessons on each expository writing element*: the five-paragraph essay, beginnings, organizing your main ideas and details, topic sentences, paragraphs, endings.

⊘ *Begin each lesson with texts (or copies of texts) that students analyze and mark up using sticky notes or colored pencils or highlighters.* If you need a simple but strong example, write a "perfect" paragraph that contains a topic sentence, main ideas, details, and a conclusion.

⊘ *Pass out texts and invite students to help you find additional examples.*

⊘ *Create a rubric for each element.* Have the class help you list what makes a good beginning, topic sentence, main idea, detail, or ending.

⊘ *Introduce cool tools*—highlighter tape, highlighters, colored pencils, clear acetate to place over pages and write on with felt-tip pens.

⊘ *Assess student progress.* Do the students need more examples of this kind of text? Can they verbalize their observations?

Modeling

⊘ *Create an example of the particular element* on a projected transparency or chart paper—a topic sentence or paragraph, for example. Think aloud as you write.

OR

⊘ *Over a series of days, write a complete report on a particular topic.* Model one step of the process at a time and move to shared and guided writing. End each lesson by asking students to write the same element you modeled.

⊘ *Use everyday examples.* Write a quick essay or paragraph about why you only buy used cars, or how your family spends weekends, or about a place you've been. Anything goes! Be sure to also model how to write more serious nonfiction topics related to science and social studies.

⊘ *Check your work against the rubric or chart.* Ask students to tell what they think is important or what they liked about your model. Have you included the points listed?

⊘ *Introduce cool tools.* Throughout the lesson, check student understanding. Ask students to signal their agreement or disagreement with thumbs-up or thumbs-down signals. Have them read your example aloud together as a group.

Assess student progress. Do students need the scaffolding you provide in shared writing or are they ready to work more independently in a guided writing group?

Shared Writing

Mix shared and guided writing throughout the lesson. Serve as a recorder for the class or a small group, writing down what they dictate. Ask probing questions and prompt students to include details. Then switch to guided writing, letting groups write on their own with your assistance. Combine the students' guided writing and the shared portion. Write a conclusion together.

Introduce cool tools. During a whole-class lesson pass out index cards on which you have written transitional words such as *therefore, another point, while.* Put individual students "in charge" of these words. When writing a shared piece, stop at points that require transitions and call on students to come up to the chart and insert their index card.

OR

Encourage a volunteer to write in front of the class. If the student is a reluctant writer or English language learner, you may want to write while the student dictates.

Ask students to turn to a partner, then write a portion of the text on a cool tool or in a notebook. Then invite a volunteer to come forward and share their example and add it to the text.

Assess student progress. How did students do during the discussions? Are they ready to write on their own? Do you need to call up a small group and guide them while they write individually?

Guided Writing

Implement guided writing during a whole-class lesson. Have table groups "jigsaw" a portion of text. Put each table in charge of writing one paragraph of a five-paragraph essay. Move from group to group, guiding the discussions. Each student writes her or his individual contribution on a sentence strip or piece of adding machine tape; the group then puts the pieces in order and tapes them to a larger sheet of paper. Collect, combine, and display all the group products and reread as a whole class; reorder or revise as necessary. Use cool tools, such as large pieces of butcher paper, overhead transparency strips, sentence strips, a pocket chart, colorful index cards.

Implement guided writing with an intervention group of reluctant or struggling writers. Meet with the group from time to time to practice a skill or for a few days or a week to write a complete report together. If necessary remodel the writing skill or element you are teaching. Give each student in the group a portion of text to write. If necessary conduct part of the lesson as a shared writing. Lead the group in rereading the material chorally. Reinforce the importance of crossing out text and rewriting it. Use cool tools: brads, yarn, rings, index cards, sentence strips, clear acetate, giant pieces of colorful paper, tiny sticky notes.

✐ *Implement guided writing with temporary needs groups.* While the rest of the class is writing individually, meet with groups of students who are having difficulty with a particular stage of writing (topic sentences, supporting details). Spot-teach or remodel.

✐ *Add to the class rubric for expository writing.* (See Appendix D)

✐ *Assess student progress.* Can students now work independently, or do they need to continue to meet in a group?

Independent Writing

✐ *Encourage students to refer to the group experiences they have shared.*

✐ *Assess student progress.* Do they apply what they have learned from modeled/ shared lessons in their own writing? Do they need more work in guided groups?

Guided Conferring

✐ *Have students read their work to one another in small groups and use the class rubric as a guideline for compliments and suggestions.*

✐ *Use hallway scoring.* Hang or display each collaborative group's completed report. Have students check off on a scoring sheet (see Figure 6.14) whether it meets the criteria on the rubric. Another option is to have students write compliments or questions on sticky notes and post them near each piece of writing.

✐ *Conduct a gallery tour.* Have students walk slowly around the room, reading and discussing each group's finished report. Leave a comment sheet next to the report for suggestions. Have the groups revise their work based on these suggestions.

✐ *Lead a guided conference.* Conduct a roundtable discussion with seven or eight students using the following prompts:
  ✐ *Share your beginning paragraph.*
  ✐ *Share your best topic sentence.*
  ✐ *Ask the group for their help on something you are having trouble with.*

Figure 6.14

Rubric for Hallway Scoring

Read each group's minireport. Give a check mark for each element included. Add up the total number of checks. Add compliments and suggestions.

Name of Scorer _____

Group # _____   Score _____

Title _____

Introduction
❑ Catchy beginning
❑ Circle one: quote, create a scene, fact, opinion, question(s), dialogue, pose a problem

❑ Thesis statement:
❑ Includes preview of paragraphs below

Paragraph #1
❑ Topic sentence
❑ Detail supports topic
❑ Detail supports topic
❑ Detail supports topic

Paragraph #2
❑ Topic sentence
❑ Detail supports topic
❑ Detail supports topic
❑ Detail supports topic

Paragraph #3
❑ Topic sentence
❑ Detail supports topic
❑ Detail supports topic
❑ Detail supports topic

Ending/Conclusion
❑ Circle one: question, simple wrap-up, create a scene, warning or invitation to do something, quotation
❑ Restates thesis in a new way (reread first paragraph to check this)

Compliments:

Suggestions/Comments/Questions:

Total Number of Checks_____

Rubric for Hallway Scoring

Read each group's minireport. Give a check mark for each element included. Add up the total number of checks. Add compliments and suggestions.

Name of Scorer _____

Group # _____   Score _____

Title _____

Introduction
❑ Catchy beginning
❑ Circle one: quote, create a scene, fact, opinion, question(s), dialogue, pose a problem

❑ Thesis statement:
❑ Includes preview of paragraphs below

Paragraph #1
❑ Topic sentence
❑ Detail supports topic
❑ Detail supports topic
❑ Detail supports topic

Paragraph #2
❑ Topic sentence
❑ Detail supports topic
❑ Detail supports topic
❑ Detail supports topic

Paragraph #3
❑ Topic sentence
❑ Detail supports topic
❑ Detail supports topic
❑ Detail supports topic

Ending/Conclusion
❑ Circle one: question, simple wrap-up, create a scene, warning or invitation to do something, quotation
❑ Restates thesis in a new way (reread first paragraph to check this)

Compliments:

Suggestions/Comments/Questions:

Total Number of Checks_____

Figure 6.15

Possible Expository Writing Minilessons Focusing on the Six Traits

Ideas

- *What's your point?* Preview the text. Have students write what they wonder about the topic on sticky notes. Help students categorize their "wonderments" into their 3 or 4 main report points.

- *It's in the book.* Ask students to build their main report points and supporting details on the headings in the text.

Word Choice

- *Don't just sit there!* Type up a brief shared/guided report the class wrote. Make copies for all students. Ask students to circle all passive verbs. Tell them to eliminate *is, am, was, were, have, has.* Create a list of more active verbs that fit the topic and have students, in teams, reword and rewrite to avoid the outlawed words.

- *Change the Verbs race.* Have table groups race to change verbs from passive to active.

Organization

- *What color is your paragraph?* (Auman 2006). Assign colors to portions of a paragraph. Choose one color for the topic sentence and other colors for main ideas and details. Have students write parts of a paragraph in the appropriate colors and put their colorful paragraphs together.

- *Transition, transition, who's got the transition?* Pass out four to six cards with transitional words and phrases on them—*as well as, next, due to,* etc. When revising the group pieces, have the student "in charge" of each transition word or phrase stand up when it is needed.

Sentence Fluency

- *Breathe, breathe, breathe.* Ask a student to read slowly from an expository text. Have her or him take a deep breath at the beginning of each sentence and (rather dramatically, exaggerating) expel any breath remaining at the end of each sentence. This breathy reading demonstrates sentence length. Does your report include both longer and shorter sentences?

- *Sentence elaboration.* Choose one dull sentence and have table teams rewrite it into a more interesting sentence.

Voice

- *Who is it?* As a class, write an imaginary journal entry for a nonfiction topic (you serve as the scribe). Then ask pairs of students to write entries (e.g. as a planet, explorer, or animal) and share.

- *Silent conversations.* Have a silent conversation with students. Role-play as characters from history. Write your responses and comments on the overhead and have students respond on their slates. Have student pairs try it.

Conventions

- *Pass the period, please!* Bring in empty salt and pepper shakers and spice containers. Label the containers with the words and symbols for period, question mark, capital, comma, etc. Give the containers to student volunteers. As someone reads the text and one of the "ingredients" is needed, the student who has that container "sprinkles" the punctuation.

Figure 6.16

A Five-Paragraph Essay Frame

Introduction

Catchy first sentence

Thesis statement

Sneak Preview (list three topics)

Topic #1

Topic sentence

Detail

Detail

Detail

Conclusion

Topic #2

Topic sentence

Detail

Detail

Detail

Conclusion

Topic #3

Topic sentence

Detail

Detail

Detail

Conclusion

Close

Catchy sentence

Restate thesis statement

Review sneak preview

Discussion Questions

1. What do your students have trouble with when writing expository texts or reports? What is hard about teaching expository writing? Do your students like this type of writing?

2. What are some common beginnings students use when writing expository texts? (*In this report I will tell you about. . . .*) What are some common endings? (*So that is my report about. . . .*) How do students benefit from identifying beginnings/endings in real texts first? How can guided writing lessons help you improve your students' use of beginnings and endings in expository texts?

3. Design an everyday think-aloud (like the one in which I told of Rebecca's day at home sick) that you can use with students. After trying it with your class, tell the group how it helped the students understand expository text structure. Share more ideas for everyday think-alouds with your colleagues.

4. How does using Katie Wood Ray's chart (see Chapter 5) help teach the identifying examples portion of the lessons in this chapter? How can students use highlighters and colored pencils during this step of the lesson to enhance learning?

5. The guided writing reports in this chapter had interesting topics like sharks and the *Titanic*. What topics might your students be interested in that you could research and then write about in guided groups? What topics have worked in the past for your grade level?

Try It in Your Classroom

- Try a variety of cool tools during the guided portion of your lessons. Compare how students respond to writing on transparencies, large pieces of construction paper, or sentence strips. Which do you prefer? Why?

- Ask students to all write beginnings for the same topic. Assign a different beginning to each table group. Share.

- Meet with an intervention group for at least one week for fifteen minutes a day. Write a piece of expository text together. Use shared writing for some portions of the text and guided writing in which each student writes on a sentence strip and adds to the whole. What worked? How did small-group instruction impact the writing of these students? How many times a year will you do this?

- Try hallway scoring (see page 105). What do you notice?

Chapter Seven

Lights, Camera, Action!
Acting Out
Narratives

Writing is something you use to tell about things that are important to you. You can write your stories down and they stay there.

—Callie

Maybe you recall participating in plays, readers theatre, and puppet shows when you were a student in elementary school. When I first began teaching, my students acted out the stories we read. We wrote our own plays to perform for the parents and other classes. The students dressed up in costumes, donned funny masks, and made elaborate puppets and sets. Sometimes we acted out our plays on in both Spanish and English. What happened? These days it seems we just don't have time in our standards-oriented, skills-based, testing-driven classrooms to include everything. Over the years other, more "important" lessons have taken over; there isn't time for drama.

The good news is that drama is making its way back to classrooms everywhere! Research tells us that fluency is critical to success in reading and comprehension (Rasinski 2003). When students take part in drama activities of any sort, they re-read texts many times for a purpose and their reading rate improves. Our English language learners especially benefit from the vocabulary reinforcement that drama provides. Drama is too beneficial to skip.

Vivian Paley, a brilliant early childhood researcher and educator, first created story plays to use with preschool and kindergarten children. I've expanded her concept to include writing lessons that you can use to motivate and excite your students at any grade level while reinforcing critical writing skills. This type of collaboration is the perfect match for guided writing lessons.

Writing Stories or Personal Narratives

Students often find writing a "story" a challenge. Although they read mostly fiction in school, they often are stumped when they are asked to write their own. Here are some common problems associated with writing stories or, in the case of older students, personal narratives:

- ✐ Students have difficulty beginning their story.

- ✐ Students present a problem and then solve it too quickly.

- ✐ Students have trouble developing the plot—the get stuck on what comes next.

✐ Students forget to weave in actions, feelings, dialogue, and thoughts as they develop their plots (Mariconda 1999).

✐ Students rarely want to revise their work.

Do you remember as a child setting up pretend scenarios? I recall sitting on the lawn surrounded by all the neighborhood kids talking loudly and all at once:

This time let's pretend that Captain Hook is coming to get us and we'll mix quicksand to try to capture him.

Let's say we live on the porch and we can pretend it is our tree house with Tinker Bell.

I think we should hide from Captain Hook in the bushes.

Somehow we came to a consensus and pretended up a storm for a few barefoot hours on a hot summer evening. Whether our improvisations featured a tricycle traffic jam or the adventurous Peter Pan or (dare I tell?) a kissing bandit, we were lost in the imaginary worlds of our exciting stories.

Young children come to school bursting with creativity and stories. Even my two middle school–age children still occasionally pretend when they entertain my second grader at home. They crawl under the dining room table with her and make a couch-cushion fort where they can hide from the monsters or spy on the enemy. A child's imagination is vivid and engaging. If only we could tap into that excitement when it is time to write at school.

Story plays are innovative enactments spontaneously written and cast by children. Vivian Paley, who taught kindergarten for thirty-seven years (mostly at the University of Chicago's lab school) and has written numerous books on her research in early childhood, developed this child-centered activity based on her observations of children playing. She believes that children's "work" is their play and that when given the opportunity, they emerge as natural and ingenious actors. In her approach to story plays, a child dictates a story to his or her teacher, who serves as scribe. Then the "playwright" casts his or her story play with classmates. As the teacher reads the child's story aloud, the chosen actors dramatize the reading. Imagine the delight children experience, whether seeing their own ideas acted out or being chosen to star in someone else's play. Story plays engage children because they are written by and for children.

I first heard about story plays from my dear friend Ellen. Her son attended a preschool where the children participated in these child-centered dramas. When I found out that several of my favorite veteran primary teachers use story plays, I knew I had to try them. Since then I've adapted and built on Vivian Paley's work, creating a version of story plays that encourages elementary children to improve their writing. The concept can be expanded to the intermediate grades to promote fluent creation and revision of personal narratives.

Using Story Plays

Story plays differ from other types of drama in that they are planned, composed, and dramatized by children. They're on-the-spot enactments of stories read by a narrator and require very little preparation. These impromptu dramas appeal to children of all ages and encourage joy, creativity, and imagination in students' narrative writing. After dramatizing their initial story ideas, students are ready to turn their plays into written stories filled with rich action and dialogue.

Here are the basics.

First, ask students to tell you what they know about stories and plays. A lively discussion will naturally ensue, comments about plot, characters, the stage, and an audience. Begin by calling up a few students at a time to act out story plays written by other students. Figures 7.1 through 7.3 are sample story plays you can read to your class. Choose actors for each play and don't rehearse ahead of time. Simply begin reading the story plays aloud and ask the student actors to listen carefully and perform the actions and repeat the dialogue. These unrehearsed enactments prompt laughter, smiles, and the undivided attention of the audience and cast.

After acting out a sample story play or two you might write a shared class story play or work with students in small guided groups to write collaborative versions. Have the students brainstorm, perhaps using a graphic organizer like the one in Figure 7.8, sketching quick scenes or jotting down key words. (Not writing out their story in full sentences until after they perform it means the students are more likely to revise their work.) Each group then selects a narrator to "read" the skeleton of a story and actors to dramatize it. After performing their drama and receiving feedback from an audience, each student or group writes out the story in detail. It may even be illustrated and turned into a book.

Figure 7.1

"The Little Duckling," by Ozzie, Lou, and Lindsay (third- and first-grade buddies)

Characters:
Quacky Duck
Sox the Fox
Box the Fox
Rainbow the Cat
Narrator

Once there was a duck named Quacky. There were two foxes named Sox and Box. The duck was walking to the pond to take a swim. The foxes climbed a ladder to get out of their hole.
The foxes said, "Let's make duck stew."
Then they chased the duck back into the hole.
"Run fast. Let's get him!"
A cat named Rainbow, with orange stripes and green eyes, was watching in the tree nearby. The cat jumped into the hole and stuck out her sharp claws.
Rainbow said to Quacky, "Don't worry, Rainbow is here!"
Rainbow said "Go home" to the foxes. She scared them away and saved the duck.
Quacky and Rainbow lived happily ever after.

The End

Figure 7.2

"Little Famous and the Anaconda," by Jason, Caitlin, and Bryan (third- and first-grade buddies)

Characters:
> *Little Famous*
> *Anaconda*
> *Narrator*

Episode 1: New Friends

There was an island. A lizard named Little Famous lived on the island. Then one day Little Famous was walking by the river alone.

Suddenly, an anaconda popped out and swallowed him whole.
Then he spit him out.
Little Famous yelled, "Smoogie!"
The anaconda said, "You taste awful!"
Then Little Famous said, "Let's be friends."

Episode 2: Where Did the Fish Go?

Anaconda was fishing for two weeks without as much as a nibble.
Little Famous said, "Smoogie, I would swim to Alaska, if I were you."
So Anaconda and Little Famous swam to Alaska to find their lost fish.
Anaconda caught the island fish. They were both about to freeze when Little Famous made a net out of ice. Then they swam back to the island and put the fish where they belong.

[Students often feel that this story play is funny but doesn't much make sense. After acting it out, ask students to think of ways to make it better. This is a great opportunity to talk about what makes a good story play.]

Benefits of Story Plays

- Story plays are impromptu; they don't require hours of preparation.

- Story plays allow children to capture ideas generated within their "pretend" world and eventually turn them into written stories.

- Students are forced to think about what makes sense as they act out their writing.

- Students learn to incorporate dialogue, rich description, and action in their stories.

- Students become more comfortable revising their writing.

- Students learn to expand on ideas by receiving constant feedback from peers.

- Students' organizational and creative skills improve.

Encouraging Revision in Younger Children

"Is there anything you want to change about your story? Maybe you could add some details about the setting and the beginning of your visit with your grandfather." I'm

Figure 7.3

"The Great Unknown," by Lindsay, Ann, and Jason (second graders)

Characters:
  Bird
  Horse
  Cat 1
  Cat 2
  Dragon
  Narrator

Once upon a time two black cats were playing tag in a field. They accidentally-without-thinking ran into a forest called The Great Unknown.

First the cats tried climbing up a tree to find their way out of the dark forest, but all they saw was more trees and treetops.

Then they saw a white horse and a blue bird. The cats decided to ask them how to get out of the forest.

So they asked, "How do you get out of this forest?"

The bird flew down and hopped onto the horse's back.

"Hop on," says the bird to the cats.

The whole group walked with towering spruce hanging over them. Just then they thought they saw another tree but it was a DRAGON! The dragon hopped out of the trees and cut in front of them. It was a HUGE dragon!

The dragon scooped them up in its claws and brought them to the mountains.

He set them in a cave where they almost froze to death. The dragon flew out of the cave and left the little group to die. An avalanche came and blocked the entrance to the cave.

The cats began to scratch their way out. After one hour they were free and out.

The cats asked the blue bird again, "How can we get out of the forest?"

Pointing with her feather, the blue bird said, "Straight ahead and then left."

So they all rode home on the horse's back.

---

conferring with third grader Juan during writing workshop. "Nope. I'm done," he tells me matter-of-factly. Juan, like many other elementary students, feels quite satisfied with his first attempts at writing his narrative.

Most elementary students do not want to revise their writing and for good reason. Very young children live in the moment, and their minds move quickly on to the next thing. In addition, they find the physical act of rewriting daunting; their fingers tire quickly as they grip their pencils tightly, trying to remember the necessary letter–sound associations to spell out their message. No wonder they don't want to "write" again. Older students are often no different in their attitude toward revision. They don't see value in rewriting. It's hard work. This presents challenges for us as teachers as we try to motivate our students to make changes in their text in both content and conventions. I tell students that all good writers rewrite. In fact writers should be called *rewriters*, since that is what they spend a great deal of time doing!

Figure 7.4

Rachael's Story Play Outline		
Who? *Cat* *Dolphin* *Dragon* *Snake*	Where? *Beach, rocks*	What happens first? *The cat takes a walk.*
What happens next? (Problem) *Dragon locks the animals in a cage.*	What is the ending? How is the problem solved? *Snake saves the cat.*	

This form is adapted from one created by teachers Carol Levin and Kristin Choy.

Here are some reasons why writers rewrite their stories or narratives:

🖎 to include more details

🖎 to develop an idea more fully so that it makes more sense

🖎 to delete a point or idea that is unnecessary

🖎 to add more voice through dialogue, action, description, or characters' feelings

🖎 to use better, more interesting words

Writers make changes in their texts after rereading the material for clarity and after receiving feedback from others. When students act out their stories, they very quickly realize there may be some holes in the plot line. I enjoy watching their faces as they realize there is a description or action missing. The narrator often ad-libs for a moment or two to help make sense of a flailing drama.

In first grade, Rachael once worked in a group with three boys to draw scenes for a story play about a cat, dolphin, dragon, and snake. Their original outline was quite simple and included few details (see Figure 7.4). When Rachael began to narrate, she realized the script was too bare-bones, so she filled in many details along the way: "One day Cat decided to take a walk along the beach and invited Dolphin. They walked and walked and came to a tree. . . ."

Afterward, each group member wrote a version of the story play, adding details, events, and descriptions. The dramatization led the children naturally into revision. Allowing students to dramatize before they write too much helps them clarify their ideas and see where they need to add details.

Responses to the following questions will prompt students to rewrite and add to their creations:

🖎 What did you like about our story? What works?

🖎 Did we do a good job describing the setting? Why or why not? What else could we do?

- Did the story make sense? Why or why not? What is missing?

- What could we add or take out to make it better?

- How was our beginning and ending?

- What did you think of our problem? Did we solve it too quickly? Why or why not? What could we do to fix it?

- Do you think we need to add dialogue, more action, description, or a character's feelings?

Older Students and Everyday Narratives

Older elementary students benefit from acting out story sketches as well. Try using story plays when students write personal narratives about things that have happened to them. Imagine how much fun your students will have acting out getting a finger stuck in a car door, wearing pajamas to school thinking it is PJ day when it isn't, telling a parent after losing something valuable, baby-sitting an energetic two-year-old, or taking a scary ride at an amusement park for the first time. Ask students to jot down a skeletal outline of the setting, characters, problem, and an event of two, then cast class members to act out the story as they tell it. When students see their stories played out, they easily identify the "holes" in their plot line and revise accordingly.

When a class of sixth graders I was working with tried writing story plays, I noticed that quite a few of them were just stringing dialogue together and putting very little description or narrative in between the speeches. Rachael and Lindsay's story was about getting their ears pierced. Their first effort included loads of single lines of dialogue like this:

Rachael: Lindsay, are you nervous?

Lindsay: No, not really.

Rachael: Can you go first?

Lindsay: Sure, why not?

They needed more guided instruction from me to help them incorporate more description for the narrator. When I had explained story plays, many of the students heard the word *play* and wrote just dialogue. I needed to back up and provide guided support. As a class we reread Rachael and Lindsay's draft and reworked it to include more description:

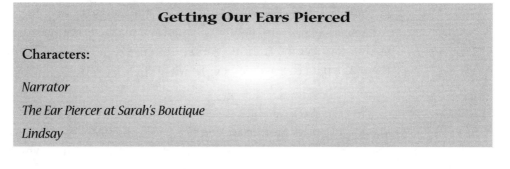

Getting Our Ears Pierced

Characters:

Narrator

The Ear Piercer at Sarah's Boutique

Lindsay

Lindsay's mom

Rachael

Rachael's mom

Lindsay and Rachael crawled up the almost vertical hill from school carrying their twenty-five-pound backpacks filled with homework. The girls hiked with excitement because Friday had finally arrived. Lindsay noticed that Rachael's step had an unusual, jubilant bounce to it.

So she asked her, "Why are you so excited?"

Rachael replied with joy, "I'm finally getting my ears pierced today! My mom made me wait twelve long years for this day."

Lindsay's face lit up. "My mom and I have been talking about getting my ears pierced, but we never actually got to it."

Rachael replied, "You should totally come with us! We could get our ears pierced together!"

So the longtime friends and neighbors skipped into Rachael's house and flung their backpacks off creating a giant thud. They consulted with both mothers, and both said yes. They all piled into the minivan for the long drive to Sarah's Boutique. The thirty-minute trek seemed like an eternity as the girls anxiously discussed the pain that they were about to endure. For the entire ride they repeated what they'd heard from their friends, comments like, "It feels like a pinch." "It feels hot afterwards." "It sounds like a stapler." "It only hurts a little." "Even babies get their ears pierced." For the entire ride they nervously pinched their ear lobes in preparation for the dreaded needle. Rachael asked a thousand times, "Will it hurt?"

They arrived at Sarah's Boutique and hunted out the expert ear piercer in the Bay Area, Marie. "Even the doctors recommend her," comforted Rachael's mom.

Lindsay offered to go first because she noticed Rachael's excruciating anxiety obvious in her face. She hopped up into the chair of doom. The expert piercer approached with a rather small gun. The amazing small size of the gun calmed the girls' nerves a little bit. The piercer held the gun up to Lindsay's ear. Lindsay grimaced. The sound of the piercing gun rang a staple sound like *poooowwching* through the girl's ears.

Lindsay said, "Ouch."

Rachael asked, "Did that hurt?"

"No, it didn't really hurt," replied Lindsay in an effort to comfort her worried friend.

Next, Rachael sat up in the chair wearing an uneasy expression. The ear piercer comforted her by telling her it wouldn't hurt a bit. *Pooowwchingg* went the gun.

Lindsay asked, "Do you think that hurt?"

"Not as much as I thought it would," Rachael replied.

Rachael's expression lightened when she realized that her ears had just been pierced. Rachael and Lindsay's ears still stung a bit afterwards, but they knew that this was a pain they would never have to endure again.

You can also have students develop scenes from their weekend webs (see Chapter 4) into story plays. Story plays don't have to be limited to personal narratives, either. You might even try acting out arguments or debates, such as why there should or shouldn't be zoos, why kids should have less homework, or the benefits of eating healthy or not smoking. Story plays might also be about things students just learned in science or social studies—the planets or the end of slavery, for example. Story plays can be about anything!

Buddy Story Plays

One of my favorite ways to teach story play writing is using cross-age tutors. Picture the fourth graders and first graders at Randall School (many of whom are English language learners) seated together on the floor ready to experience some story plays. The mood is anxious as I select the actors. I choose a smattering of both primary and intermediate students, and giggles abound. After we've acted out several stories, I ask students to form groups of four, two older students and two younger. The older students serve as scribes while the little ones dictate their ideas. I caution the fourth graders not to write the story but to put down only what the younger children say and probe with good questions like *what do you want to say next?* or *who is in your story?* We take turns acting out as many of the stories as we have time for, and the students, smiling and happy, go back to their respective classrooms.

Both classes of students have benefited from our time together. Each child returns to his or her classroom to illustrate and write the story play to bring to share next week during buddy time. Buddies are delighted to read their versions of the plays, each with its own spin, to one another.

You can also have the older buddies write story plays that feature their little buddies as characters. The authors can narrate the plays as their little buddies—playing themselves—act out the scenes. Story plays are especially effective in this setting, because every child is engaged in acting and writing for a motivating audience.

Story Play Club

Del Rey School, in Orinda, California, tried offering an after-school story play club. Students of all ages, from kindergarten through fifth grade, sign up for the hour-long weekly sessions. During the meetings, which include snacks, one older student works with two or three younger children. The older students act as scribes and help the little ones develop an interesting and sensible story. Each week the students quickly brainstorm their story ideas and take turns dramatizing them. (You could culminate your version of the club by inviting parents to a performance of the students' favorite story plays or publishing some of them, with illustrations, in book form and placing them in the school or classroom library.)

Story Plays with Kindergartners

The little band of six kindergartners sits quietly on their squares on the carpet in front of me. (During work centers this week, each group will meet with me to create story plays in a guided setting. It will take all week to get to every group.) Eager to be called on, all hands go up when I ask for volunteers to help draw and act out the story we just composed together. I've drawn three boxes on a chart and labeled them *beginning*, *middle*, and *end*. Student volunteers draw pictures of our story on the chart, and I write key words to help them remember the action or dialogue. We write about a hungry girl and boy, Juana and Ramon, who see the cookies on top of the refrigerator but can't reach them. In the middle of the story the duo try standing on a chair, then a stool, but they still they can't reach the cookies. Finally, their big brother, Fernando, enters the kitchen; he puts Juana on his shoulders, she grabs the cookies, and they all munch them with milk.

After our sketch of the play is complete, I give students papers folded in thirds that are also labeled *beginning*, *middle*, and *end* and ask them each to compose their own story play with drawings and labels. I guide and prompt as they think of ideas. Several of their stories look a lot like the cookie story we just acted out. To help generate original ideas instead of copying our guided piece, I stop the lesson and ask the group to help me list ideas for other story plays they could write. Two students ask for a new piece of paper as new inspirations hit. Over the course of the week, I call on students to come up and "read" their drawings and stories while other students act out the parts. The young playwrights experience the joy of creation, knowing they will be asked to share their stories with an audience and have them acted out by their peers.

Scaffolded lesson

A Story Play Lesson in Action

The first graders stream in after lunch with springtime, sun-kissed cheeks and sweaty brows. They gather quietly on the rug. I write the words *story play* on the board and underline just the word *story*. I tell them I know they've read many stories and already know a lot about how good stories are put together. Then I ask them to turn to a partner and discuss the question *what is a story?* Then we discuss this as a class. Students tell me that stories have a setting and characters. Someone else chimes in that they usually have a problem too. They name some favorite stories (some, of course, are movies).

Next I underline the word *play* and ask, "What is a play?" After again first turning to a partner, we discuss the term. They tell me that someone acts and wears a costume. There is an audience and a stage. Children eagerly share the names of plays they've been in or seen. Finally I pose my big question: "You know what a story is and you know what a play is, so what is a story play?" The room is silent. One boy raises his hand. "I think it is a story you act out into a play." Nobody else offers a response.

Sharing Examples

I tell them we'll decide whether he is correct by looking at an example that has been written by children like themselves. I pick a story play written by some first- and third-grade buddies (see Figure 7.1). "The play is called 'The Little Duckling' and was written by Ozzie, Lou, and Lindsay. Who would like to be Quacky the Duck?" Hands shoot up and I pick volunteers to be Quacky and the other characters—Sox the Fox, Box the Fox, and Rainbow the Cat. The little row of actors stands in front of the class waiting anxiously for me to read the story play aloud. What have they gotten themselves into? They smile sheepishly as I begin reading, "Once there was a duck named Quacky. There were two foxes named Sox and Box. The duck was walking to the pond to take a swim. . . ." The novice actors get the idea and make dramatic movements, repeat dialogue after I read it, and generally ham it up. The audience is delighted and responds accordingly, giggling and smiling during the entire two-minute performance. The plot continues with the foxes trying to make duck stew. They chase Quacky into his hole. Rainbow the Cat saves the day by scaring away the foxes. After the quick performance we discuss what the students liked about it. They loved the action most of all. We also list on the board that the story play has characters, a setting, problem, action, and dialogue.

Modeling/Shared Writing

As I begin to model how to compose a story play, I decide to involve students in the process. Working together we create the graphic organizer shown in Figure 7.5.

Guided Writing in Cooperative Teams

The students now work at their tables, brainstorming and sketching their own story plays. Since the class has studied marine life recently, the story plays focus on ocean settings and problems creatures might encounter in the sea. I circulate, offering guidance: *Do you think your play makes sense? Might you need to add or delete parts?* The beauty of story plays is the opportunities students have to revise their thinking. Each team performs for the class, and students offer suggestions and compliments.

Figure 7.5

Story Play Graphic Organizer

Story Play Title ___*A Home for Hermit Crab*___

Characters/Cast:
  Narrator—India
  Hermit Crab—Freddy
  Turtle—Sara
  Hermit Crab's friends—David, James, Remmy

Setting: *the sea, tide pool, rock*

Beginning	Problem	Event 1	Event 2/ Solve Problem	Ending
Hermit Crab lives in the sea.	He doesn't have anywhere to live.	He moves to a rock but a turtle lives there. Turtle is angry and snaps at him.	He moves to a tide pool.	He has his other hermit crab friends over for a dinner of BBQ seaweed and they dance.

We begin to create a story play checklist for students to use when writing future story plays:

❏ setting with description

❏ introduction of characters so we know who they are

❏ a problem that is explained and developed

❏ events that lead to solving the problem but not right away

❏ some action

❏ some talking

❏ transitions that make sense and are in order (like *next* or *then*)

❏ an ending

Scaffolded lesson

SCAFFOLDED Story Play Lessons

Story plays appeal to students of all ages. By acting out their narratives and stories, students discover what they need to work on to develop their ideas and plot. Students feel compelled to revise. Once you've modeled, feel free to allow students to jump in and write on their own while you offer support as needed.

Objectives

✐ Students identify elements they can use to develop their plots: dialogue, description, action, and characters' feelings.

✐ Students create story plays in small-group guided writing lessons using a class-created rubric that lists the story play elements.

✐ Students revise their story play after acting it out to improve ideas, transitions, and plot.

✐ Students develop better plots and organize them more effectively.

Identifying Examples

✐ *Ask students to help you analyze a story play, play, or narrative.* Use a story play in this book or a short excerpt from some other source.

✐ *Begin a class chart or rubric that includes the story elements you want to teach:* beginning, action, transitions, dialogue, description, characters' feelings, ending. (See Appendix D for a sample rubric for story plays.)

✐ *Read the story play aloud while several students dramatize it.* Analyze the elements and how they work and encourage students to use those same elements of a good story in their own story plays. Demonstrate beginnings, endings, plot development, description.

- *Introduce cool tools.* Ask students to hold up cue cards (see Figure 7.6) labeled *action, dialogue, description,* and *characters' feelings/thoughts* when examples of each occur. Which of the four elements are used most often? Which could be added? (Adapted from Mariconda 1999)

- *Assess student progress.* Do the students understand what makes a good story play? Do they need another example?

Modeling

- *Tell students the procedural steps for a story play* (see Figure 7.7). Let students in on the secret of writing a good story play. Tell them you will model all three in this lesson.

- *Brainstorm your story play using a planning chart* (see Figure 7.8). Emphasize that a story play needs a problem to solve and plenty of action and some dialogue, since it is a drama. Also include description and characters' feelings or thoughts. Use sketches and brief sentences to get your ideas down. *What should I write next? Which of my ideas fits here? This works. This doesn't work.* Only write a word or sentence or two in each section of the chart.

- *Narrate your story as volunteers act it out.* Using your bare-bones chart as a guide, tell your story, ad-libbing and filling in the gaps. Think aloud about what makes sense. Remind students that when you rewrite the story play, you will add these new details. Tell them that acting the story out helps you clarify your writing.

- *Write your story play.* Return to the chart and add the changes that occurred during the dramatization.

- *Narrate the revised version of your story.* Call on volunteer actors to perform the story play again. Is it better? How? What else could you add?

- *Check your story play against the rubric or chart.* Ask students to tell what they think is important or what they liked about your model. Add any new points they make.

- *Introduce cool tools.* Throughout the lesson stop and check student understanding via thumbs-up or thumbs-down signals. "Does this make sense?" "Do I need more action [dialogue, description, characters' thoughts or feelings]?"

- *Assess student progress.* Are students ready to write on their own after seeing you model? Are they in the mood to write? Do they need a shared writing step, or can you have guided groups write their own story plays?

Shared Writing

- *If your students need more practice internalizing the story play concept, write a shared piece together.* Have students help brainstorm the story, and record their responses on the planning chart.

Figure 7.6

Story Play Cards

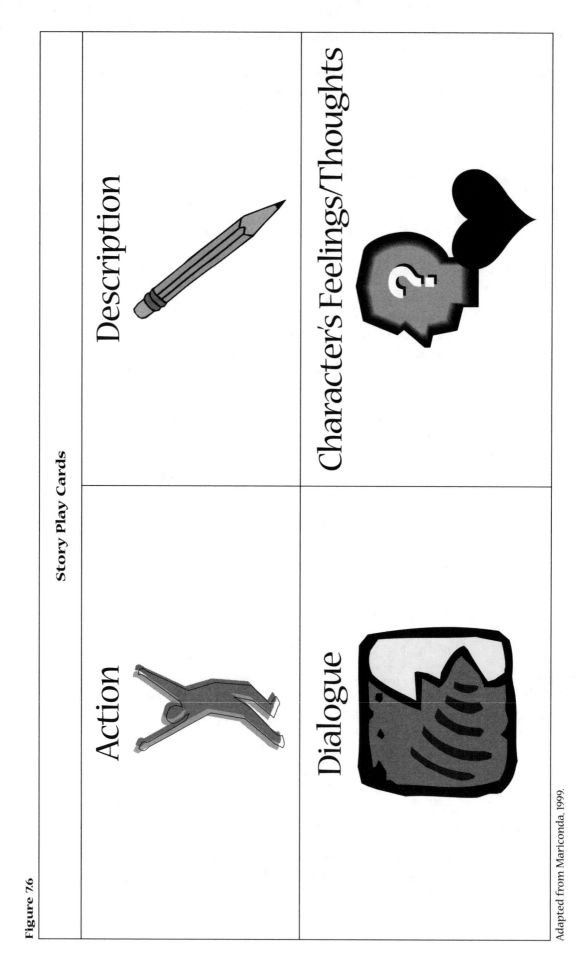

Action	Description
Dialogue	**Character's Feelings/Thoughts**

Adapted from Mariconda, 1999.

Figure 7.7

Steps in Writing a Story Play

1. Brainstorm plot ideas here or on a chart.

Setting (Where?)	Characters (Who?)	Problem (What?)	Episodes (What?)	Ending (Solve problem how?)
			1. 2. 3.	

2. Choose actors to act out your story while you tell it.

3. Revise your story based on what your audience tells you. Where do you need to add or take away? Have you included:

   Action?

   Description?

   Dialogue?

   Characters' feelings or thoughts?

Figure 7.8

Story Play Plan

1. Draw sketches and write some words, phrases, or a sentence or two about your story play.

2. Choose a narrator and actors. The narrator will use the pictures and written words to help tell the story while the actors act out the parts.

3. Revise your story play. What else do you need for it to make sense? Did you include action, description, characters' thoughts or feelings, and dialogue? (Mariconda 1999)

Story Play Title _____

Characters/Cast:

Beginning				
Problem	Event 1	Event 2	Event 3/ Solve Problem	Ending

✐ *Choose volunteers to act out the story.* The rest of the class can help you tell the story (let volunteers narrate different segments) and fill in details. Record these enhancements on the chart. Be sure to watch for and add transitions.

✐ *Write out the story, either as a class or in small groups.* (You could skip writing the new version and move on to writing new story plays in guided groups.)

✐ *Introduce cool tools.* Use puppets (sock, stick, bag, finger, or commercially made) to dramatize the story. Ask students to contribute words or sentences to your shared piece by writing their ideas on sticky notes or slates and then holding them up. Have them read their suggestions aloud. Discuss them and select some to add to the shared writing.

✐ *Assess student progress.* How did students do during the discussions and the dramatization? Can they recognize when a story play doesn't make sense? Do they add appropriate details? Do they need more shared experiences before they attempt to write story plays on their own?

Guided Writing

✐ *Implement guided writing during whole-class lessons.* Meet with table groups while they brainstorm their story play on a transparency or a chart. Remind them to act out their play for the class first and rewrite it after hearing their classmates' responses and suggestions. Ask students to think about whether their story plays include enough action, dialogue, description, and characters' thoughts or feelings.

✐ *Form a story play club during writing workshop.* Make story plays an option during writing workshop. Meet with interested students, share ideas for story plays, and show them sample story plays written by other students. Encourage each student to write his or her own story play or to work with a partner. Support their work: encourage them to brainstorm first, then dramatize, and finally write.

✐ *Implement guided writing during guided reading.* After students have read a fiction or nonfiction text, lead the group in creating a play based on the text or a spin-off idea. Create a story chart together. Narrate (or have a student narrate) while the group members act out the story. Rewrite the play together, or give students cool tools (index cards, large pieces of butcher paper, construction paper) on which to write portions of the text alone or with a partner. Support the individuals or pairs as they work. Put all the pieces of the story play together and dramatize it again. Does the story make sense? What do they need to add? Are transitions missing?

✐ *Assess student progress.* Can students now work independently or do they need to continue to work in a group? Does their writing reflect the changes that took place when the story was being acted out?

Figure 7.9

Options for Implementing Story Plays in Groups

Students can work in pairs or teams to create their story play.
They can star in their plays or call on volunteers.

Alone
Individual students can write, cast, and narrate their own story plays. Afterward have students revise and edit their work in groups.

Everyday Topics
Keep an ongoing list of story play ideas in the classroom. Encourage students, in addition to picking make-believe, whimsical plots, to base story plays on personal narratives like the ones they write about in their weekend webs (see Chapter 4): losing a tooth, learning to play a sport or ride a bike, moving, getting lost, breaking or losing a favorite toy.

Dictation
Younger children can dictate their story plays to an adult or volunteer. If the child can't read the story play on her or his own, the adult can be the narrator and the child can direct or take part in the enactment.

Cross-Age Tutors
Have several primary-age children work with an older buddy who serves as scribe.

Once a Week
Work with one group each week. Create a story play and perform it that same day.

Puppets
Have students use puppets to portray the story play characters.

Follow-up
Have students illustrate their story plays and put them in the class library.
Videotape the students performing their story plays and show them on parent night.
Have students create additional story plays, either original works or innovations based on another story.

Figure 7.10

Possible Story Play Minilessons Focusing on the Six Traits

Ideas

- Focus on details. After students dramatize a shared story play for the first time, divide students into teams. Ask each team to focus on one aspect of adding detail (description, action, dialogue, characters' feelings or thoughts) and act it out for the group. Which type of detail works best for this story play?

Word Choice

- During a modeled writing lesson, write *said* every time a character speaks. Ask students what they notice. Someone should say, "Too many *saids*." Cross them out and select stronger words that fit the text, character, and situation.

- Make a list or chart of synonyms for *said*. Have students add words they encounter in their reading to the list (examples: *yelled, screamed, whispered, questioned, added, demanded, coaxed, pleaded, sighed, offered, explained*).

Organization

- Create a story play in a subgenre:
  mystery
  sitcom
  game show
  reality show
  folktale or fairy tale.

- Try different types of beginnings (dialogue, a "noisy" word, feelings and thoughts, action) and endings (a quote, a thought, a question).

- If your students' story plays end too soon, use the Third Time Is a Charm strategy (see Figure 5.3).

Sentence Fluency

- Do the sentences sound natural when read aloud? Do any need to be reworked?

- Are some sentences longer and others shorter?

- Does the dialogue sound natural?

Voice

- Act out a story play using different voices that reflect the characters' personalities and moods. How does voice, or even tone of voice impact the presentation of the play?

- Use scary, mean, mad, sweet voices to create a mood as you read a story play.

Conventions

- Check to see whether the students' dialogue uses quotation marks, commas, and capital letters correctly. Have partners edit the dialogue in their story plays.

- Have students look in books to see how authors write dialogue. What do they notice?

Independent Writing

🖉 *When students are ready to write their own story play, remind them to use the class-created rubric as they work.*

🖉 *Assess student progress.* Do students apply what they learned during the modeled and shared writing lessons? Do they brainstorm, act out, and revise? Collect and analyze examples of student work. Do they need to work in guided groups again?

Guided Conferring

🖉 *Have students read and act out their story plays in small groups.* Rotate from group to group or call up one group at a time to meet with you. Use the rubric (class-created or from Appendix D) as a guideline for compliments and suggestions.

Discussion Questions

1. What is a story play? How are story plays different from other plays you've done with your students? What appeals to you? What will appeal to your students?

2. What do you remember about pretending and using your imagination as a child? Discuss the role of pretending in children's development. How can we unlock students' imaginations? What if your students are avid video game players? How can you help them unleash their imaginations?

3. Ask students to act out stories before writing them out in detail. How does the acting step force students to revise? What are some examples of revision you saw taking place on the spot? How are the written story plays different from the original brainstormed and dramatized versions?

4. What are some creative ways to use story plays with older students? Cross-age buddies? A story play club? How do your English language learners respond to story plays?

5. After a whole-class lesson, break students into teams to brainstorm story plays about something that really happened to them. What kinds of scenarios do students come up with? Do the topics vary? How can you encourage a variety of ideas for story plays?

Try It in Your Classroom

🖉 Choose a story play in this chapter and read it to your class. Invite students to act out the story as you go along. Ask them to discuss what a story play is. Write a shared story play using an everyday event that happened to one of your students recently. (Look to their weekend webs for ideas.) What did you learn? What do the students need to work on? Did they grasp the story play concept?

✐ Ask older students to write story plays for their younger buddies that incorporate the buddies' names. As the older student narrates, the younger buddies can act out the stories playing the character that has the same name as they do. Ask the younger children to revise and add episodes, dialogue, or feelings or thoughts.

✐ Are your students able to recognize when better transitions are needed? Guide students to revise their story plays so that the transitions between events are smooth.

Appendices

Appendix A

Five Ways to Use a Flap Book in Guided Writing Lessons

Basic Directions

Use the reproducible form on the next page or a piece of plain paper. Fold the paper lengthwise and make four horizontal cuts in the top fold, creating four "flaps" or "doors" for students to label and then lift and write under.

Using a Flap Book for a Story Play

When student teams are brainstorming ideas for story plays, have them label the flaps *setting*, *characters*, *problem*, and *solution*, and sketch their ideas underneath. The narrator can use the flap book as a guide during the initial run-through. After acting out the story play, have students use the flap book as a guide as they write out their stories in full sentences.

Using a Flap Book for a Noisy Poem

Have students sketch one or two sense organs on top of each flap—eye, ear, hand, nose, or mouth—and brainstorm rich vocabulary for noisy poems under the respective flaps.

Using a Flap Book with Weekend Webs

Have students write question words on the outside of the flaps—*who*, *what*, *where*, *why*. Partners take turns telling each other about their topics. Then they exchange flap books and write questions about relevant details to include. Students can then write their entry using the questions as a guide.

Using a Flap Book for Expository Writing

Ask students to write their main ideas on the outside of the flaps—for example, *kinds of whales*, *what whales eat*, *where whales live*, *how whales survive*—and brainstorm details underneath.

Using a Flap Book for Third-Time-Is-a-Charm Technique

Have students write *setting/characters*, *problem*, *repeating events/words*, and *ending* on the four flaps. After reading several books featuring characters and events in threes, such as *The Three Little Pigs* and *The Three Billy Goats Gruff*, have students brainstorm repeating-events stories, organizing their ideas under the four flaps.

Pattern for a Flap Book

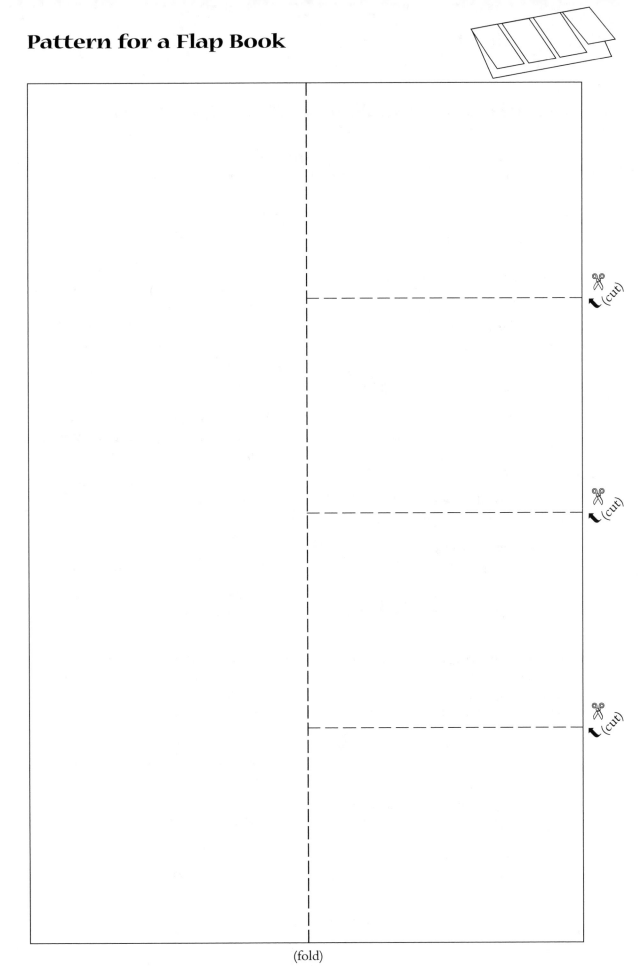

(cut)

(cut)

(cut)

(fold)

Appendix B

Creative Ways for Students to Share Their Writing

Students may, of course, share their final drafts in any of these ways. But each may also be used to share earlier drafts when students are looking for feedback on which to base revisions.

Tour Time

- Student writing teams quietly tour the other tables in the room, where the other teams' writing is on display.

- They share their reactions orally (or in writing if paper for that purpose is provided at each table).

- Students listen to or read the responses to their work and revise accordingly.

- Individual work may also be shared this way.

Stroll Line

- Students stand in two lines across from each other, their writing in hand.

- On the teacher's signal, they share their writing with the person across from them.

- Students give a compliment and ask a question or make a suggestion.

- On the teacher's signal, everyone in one line takes one step to the right (the person at the head of the line takes the space left vacant at the end).

- Students read their work to the new partner and discuss as above.

- The rotation continues until students have received feedback from several students.

- Students return to their desks and add to their writing.

Have a Ball

- Four to eight students sit in a circle. One student has a ball (or beanbag).

- The student with the ball reads his writing and tells what he likes about it and what he is having trouble with. The rest of the group offers comments and suggestions.

- The student tosses the ball to another student.

- That student reads her piece aloud and also tells what she likes and is having trouble with. The others respond.

- This continues until every student has read his or her work.

Paper Pass

- Students sit in groups of three or four.

- The teacher says, "Pass." They hand their paper to the person on their right and read the paper they receive.

- The teacher says "pass" again, and students hand the paper they are holding to the person on their right and again read the paper they receive.

- This continues until every person in the group is again holding her or his own paper.

- The group members discuss what they liked about each paper and offer suggestions.

- Students return to their desks and revise.

Minilesson: Sentence Strips

Building on Main Ideas/Details

Description

During a small-group nonfiction guided reading lesson, students each write one important thing they learned about the topic. You help the group order their sentences in a pocket chart.

Guided Writing Options

- Read Margaret Wise Brown's *The Important Book* to the group. Model writing sentences based on the pattern Brown uses in her book.

- After each student writes one important fact on a sentence strip, work as a group to write an introduction and conclusion.

- Students work in teams on large pieces of butcher paper to write their portion of text.

Possible Skills to Teach

Using text features like headings to figure out main ideas, finding topic sentences in texts, and choosing a detail or two to go with the important fact.

Example

We read a book about bats in third-grade guided reading. After we read the book, we went back to the headings and students selected which heading they wanted to be "in charge" of. Then they each wrote a sentence about the main idea in that section of text on a sentence strip. I modeled how to restate the idea in one's own words and coached individual students. Then we ordered our sentence strips in a pocket chart and read them in unison.

Minilesson: Strip Poems

Building Organization/Ideas

Description

On a strip of paper, each student writes a factual piece of information about a topic the class has studied or a descriptive phase in response to a piece of fiction the class has read. Then students get into random groups of 3–5 members and order their strips in any way that makes sense to them. They may read and perform their poem for the class.

Guided Writing Options/Possible Skills to Teach

- Work with small groups to help them order their strip poems. Ask what makes sense when ordering the phrases. Students should defend the order they choose.

- Help students determine how they will perform their poem:
    - One student reads.
    - They read in unison (choral reading).
    - Students create movement or sound effects to accompany the reading.

Example

After reading about the rain forest, a class created rain forest strip poems. They began all lines, "In the rain forest . . . ," to which they added a poetic image or fact.

Minilesson: Daily Sentence Elaboration

Sentence Fluency and Word Choice

Description

Each day, give students a different dull short sentence ("The car was dirty," for example). Ask them, working in guided writing teams, to dress up the sentence. Have them also write their own version of the sentence in their journal.

Options

- Write each word of a dull sentence on a card or large piece of paper. Students holding the words stand in order. As a group, students write other words on cards to embellish the sentence, and students holding those cards take their appropriate places. (Spivey 1993)

- Students act out the sentences.

- Tables or teams project their embellished sentences on a transparency or display it on the whiteboard or a chart. The class votes on a favorite.

- Students take turns making up the daily dull sentence for the class to fix up.

Possible Skills to Teach

Vivid verbs, adjectives, adverbs; show-not-tell descriptions; similes, metaphors; clauses; appositives.

Examples

The girl cried.
The girl got so frustrated with her homework that she began to weep.

(Caie, 4ᵗʰ grader)

The girl sang.
One lovely girl led the chorus through "America the Beautiful."

(Caie, 4ᵗʰ grader)

Sample Dull Sentences

She sat on gum.
They came home.
The car was dirty.
The pizza was good.
He ran.
The desk was clean.
He slept.
They yelled.
Her teeth hurt.
It stopped.
The house was empty.

Six-Trait Minilesson: What a Character!

Background on Representing the Six Traits as Characters

I first began impersonating strategies in my reading lessons. I came to class dressed as *Paula the Powerful Predictor, Quincy the Questioner, Clara the Clarifier*, and *Sammy the Summarizer*. I did my think-alouds in character, and the students always remembered my teaching point. Even students in sixth grade enjoyed this kind of silliness. Because the reading characters made such an enormous impact on children, I decided to create characters for the six writing traits as well.

Description

Bring in props and costume elements that will help you create the characters described below (see The Six-Trait Team). At appropriate points in the lesson, think aloud as one of the characters. (I especially like using the characters during editing and revising sessions.)

Guided Writing Options

✎ Have student teams make posters depicting the characters and present them to the class as they describe how each character helps us write.

✎ Role-play one character per lesson to teach the students the traits.

✎ Keep props and/or posters out for students to refer to as they write.

✎ If you don't feel comfortable acting out the characters, let the props become metaphors for the traits. For example, a flashlight can symbolize finding ideas in writing.

Introducing . . .

The Six Trait Team!

 Izzy Idea

Izzy carries a flashlight around that switches on when he or she has an idea. Izzy also carries a notebook, talks fast, and chews gum rapidly. Izzy brainstorms by webbing and making lists of all his or her ideas. Sometimes Izzy focuses on thinking of details too.

 Winnie Word Wizard

Winnie does word "makeovers" by waving her or his magic wand. Dull words suddenly become colorful and action packed.

Connie Convention Cook

Connie likes to cook up the perfect dish. She or he brings salt and pepper shakers and spice containers labeled with important writing conventions, such as periods, commas, and capitals, and stirs the pot, hunting for misspelled words to strain out and spell correctly. The result is a perfect piece of writing ready to be served to the public.

 Sam Sentence Slayer

Sam has a plastic (or rubber) sword. As Sam reads a text, she or he slashes ones that are too long. Sam adds to ones that are phrases rather than sentences. When all the sentences begin the same, Sam slashes the beginning word and comes up with a new one in its place.

Val Voice

Val enjoys using a microphone to change his or her voice while reading. Val reads with emotion in a small voice, a loud, booming voice, or an accent that fits the text. *Whose voice is it?* is Val's favorite game. Val helps students learn about finding their own voice as an author.

 Ollie Organizer

Ollie, a professional home organizer, rearranges and orders things. Ollie uses a clipboard to sketch organizing ideas. He or she puts stories and reports in an order that makes sense.

Appendix D

Informal Assessment Rubrics

Throughout this book it is suggested that you work with your class to create child-centered rubrics. The students tell you what is important in a certain type of writing and together you create criteria. You may select some of these points to use in the rubric you build with your class. The rubrics serve as guides before, during, and after writing as you confer with students individually and in small guided groups.

Rubric for Noisy Poems

Quality Writing Trait	Excellent 4	Good 3	Developing 2	Beginning 1
Ideas	• focused topic • details, elaboration • literary elements like similes, metaphors, or personification	• mostly focused topic • some details • some similes, metaphors, or personification	• topic not totally focused • a few details; needs more • few if any similes, metaphors, or personification	• topic too broad • not enough details • no similes, metaphors, or personification
Organization	• interesting beginning • middle flows in logical order • interesting ending	• good beginning • middle flows fairly clearly; some revising needed • nice ending	• weak beginning • middle meanders • weak ending	• no beginning • middle unorganized; no direction • no ending
Voice	• humor or emotion • several personal experiences or opinions	• some humor or some personal experiences or opinions	• little or no humor or emotion • few or no personal experiences or opinions	• no humor or emotion • no personal experiences or opinions
Word Choice	• show-not-tell language; reader can visualize • noisy words • strong verbs • strong adjectives • alliteration	• some show-not-tell language • some noisy words • some strong verbs, adjectives • some alliteration	• little show-not-tell language • few if any noisy words • many weak verbs, adjectives • no alliteration	• no show-not-tell language • no noisy words • almost all weak verbs, adjectives • no alliteration
Fluency	• phrases, words (no sentences) • word, line, phrase repetition • varied line breaks • poetic, musical language	• many phrases, words (not all sentences) • some word, line, phrase repetition • some varied line breaks • some poetic, musical language	• lines more like sentences; no variety in length • little if any word, line, phrase repetition • lines all same length; no variety • not much poetic, musical language	• all sentences; no poetic phrasing • no word, line, phrase repetition • no poetic or musical language
Conventions	• correct spellings • looks like a poem (line breaks)	• many correct spellings • looks like a poem	• some misspellings • doesn't look like a poem throughout	• many misspellings • doesn't resemble a poem

Rubric for Weekend Webs

Quality Writing Trait	Excellent 4	Good 3	Developing 2	Beginning 1
Ideas	• web includes four or more ideas • focus idea includes four details • web entry focuses on one topic/event and includes details	• web includes three or more ideas • focus idea includes three details • web entry mostly focuses on one event or topic and includes some details	• web has two or fewer ideas • focus idea includes two or fewer details • web entry is loosly based on one topic or event	• web has no ideas • no focus idea with details • web entry is not focused on one topic or event
Organization	• interesting beginning • middle flows in logical order • interesting ending	• good beginning • middle flows fairly clearly; some revising needed • nice ending	• weak beginning • middle meanders • weak ending	• no beginning • unorganized; no direction • no ending
Voice	• humor or emotion • personality shines through • personal experiences or opinions • some dialogue	• some humor or emotion • some personality comes through • some personal experiences or opinions • some dialogue	• little or no humor or emotion • only a hint of personality comes through • few if any personal experiences or opinions • little dialogue	• no humor or emotion • stilted; no personality comes through • no personal experiences or opinions; generic • no dialogue
Word Choice *yelled* ~~said~~	• show-not-tell language; reader can visualize • strong verbs • strong adjectives • quite descriptive	• some show-not-tell language • some strong verbs, adjectives • somewhat descriptive	• little show-not-tell language • weak verbs, adjectives • not much description	• no show-not-tell language • weak verbs, adjectives • little if any description
Fluency	• sentences vary in length • sentences begin in different ways	• some variety in sentence length • most sentences begin in different ways	• little variety in sentence length • many sentences begin the same way	• no variety in sentence length • all sentence begin the same way
Conventions	• misspelled words circled • attention paid to punctuation	• some misspelled words circled • some attention paid to punctuation	• few misspelled words circled • little attention paid to punctuation	• no misspelled words circled • no attention paid to punctuation

Rubric for Reports/Expository Text

Quality Writing Trait	Excellent 4	Good 3	Developing 2	Beginning 1
Ideas	• many "wonderings," organized into categories • main ideas and details	• some "wonderings," some organized into categories • some main ideas and details	• few "wonderings," hardly any organized into categories • weak main ideas • few details	• few "wonderings," none organized into categories • very weak main ideas • very few details
Organization	• interesting expository beginning • introductory paragraph with catchy beginning and a strong preview and thesis statement • paragraphs with topic sentences, details • effective transitions • nonfiction text features • interesting expository ending	• somewhat interesting beginning • introductory paragraph with good beginning, preview, and thesis statement • most paragraphs with topic sentences, details • some effective transitions • some nonfiction text features • somewhat interesting ending	• weak beginning • introductory paragraph lacking one or two elements (catchy beginning, preview, and thesis statement) • weak topic sentences for paragraphs, not many details • few transitions • few nonfiction text features • weak ending	• very weak beginning • introductory paragraph is lacking two or more elements (catchy beginning, preview, and thesis statement) • topic sentences are inconsistent and weak, few if any details • few or no transitions • no nonfiction text features • very weak ending
Voice	• sounds like expository text (a bit formal) • some pizzazz, with interesting facts • includes "human" element	• most of it sounds like expository text • some interesting facts • some "human" element	• inconsistent expository style • personal opinions • few interesting facts • little "human" element	• weak expository style • too much opinion • few if any interesting facts • no "human" element
Word Choice *yelled said*	• strong verbs • few passive verbs (is, am, are, was, were) • strong adjectives • good description	• some strong verbs and adjectives • some passive verbs • some description	• many weak verbs and adjectives • fair number of passive verbs • little description	• mostly weak verbs • lots of passive verbs • mostly weak adjectives • very little if any description
Fluency	• sentence length varies • sentences begin in different ways	• some variety in sentence length • most sentences begin in different ways	• little variety in sentence length • many sentences begin the same way	• no variety in sentence length • all sentences begin the same way
Conventions	• misspelled words circled • attention paid to punctuation	• some misspelled words circled • some attention paid to punctuation	• few misspelled words circled • little attention paid to punctuation	• no misspelled words circled • no attention paid to punctuation

© 2007 by Lori D. Oczkus, from *Guided Writing* (Heinemann: Portsmouth, NH).

Rubric for Story Plays

Quality Writing Trait	Excellent 4	Good 3	Developing 2	Beginning 1
Ideas	• well developed • includes details, description • interesting plot	• some ideas • in-depth plot • some details	• one or two ideas • some plot • a few details	• sketchy • no plot • no details, description
Organization	• interesting beginning • middle develops logically • may include a problem and solution • varied amounts of action, dialogue, description, character feelings • interesting ending	• good beginning • middle flows fairly clearly; some revising needed • varied amounts of action, dialogue, description, character feelings • nice ending	• weak beginning • middle meanders • leans heavily on just one or two story elements (action, dialogue, description, character feelings); others are absent • weak ending	• no beginning • unorganized; no clear direction • little or no action, dialogue, description, character feelings • no ending
Voice	• humor or emotion • personality shines through • personal experiences or opinions • some dialogue	• some humor or emotion • some personality comes through • some personal experiences or opinions • some dialogue	• little or no humor or emotion • very little personality comes through • few personal experiences or opinions • little dialogue	• no humor or emotion • stilted; no personality comes through • no personal experiences or opinions; generic
Word Choice	• show-not-tell language • strong verbs for actors to act out • strong adjectives • descriptive	• some show-not-tell language • some strong verbs, adjectives • somewhat descriptive	• little show-not-tell language • weak verbs, adjectives • some description	• no show-not-tell language • weak verbs, adjectives • very little if any description
Fluency	• sentence length vary • sentences begin in different ways • reads like a story	• some variety in sentence length • most sentences begin in different ways	• little variety in sentence length • some sentences begin the same way	• no variety in sentence length • no variety in sentence beginnings
Conventions	• misspelled words circled • attention paid to punctuation • dialogue quotation marks	• some misspelled words circled • some attention paid to punctuation • some dialogue quotation marks	• few misspellings circled • little attention paid to punctuation • few dialogue quotation marks	• no awareness of misspellings • no attention paid to punctuation • no dialogue quotation marks

Literature Cited

Amato, Carol A., and David Wenzel. 1995. *The Truth About Sharks*. Barron's Educational Young Readers Series. Hauppauge, NY: Barron's.

Barrett, Judi. 1978. *Cloudy with a Chance of Meatballs.* New York: Atheneum.

Barrett, Mary Brigid. 1994. *Sing to the Stars*. Boston: Little, Brown.

Bishop, Nic. 2000. *The Living Rain Forest*. Huntington Beach, CA: Pacific Learning.

Brown, Margaret Wise. 1949. *The Important Book*. New York: HarperCollins.

Cherry, Lynne. 1992. *A River Ran Wild*. New York: Harcourt Brace.

Dupasquier, Phillippe. 1985. *Dear Daddy*. Rpt. ed. New York: Puffin.

Gibbons, Gail. 1988. *Sunken Treasure*. New York: HarperCollins Children's.

Gray, Libba Moore. 1995. *My Mama Had a Dancing Heart.* New York: Orchard.

Halter, Marek. 2004. *Sarah.* New York: Three Rivers Press.

James, Simon. 1991. *Dear Mr. Blueberry*. New York: Margaret K. McElderry (Simon and Schuster).

Laird, Donivee Martin. 1981. *The Three Hawaiian Pigs and the Magic Shark*. Honolulu: Barnaby.

Martin, Bill Jr. 1992. *Brown Bear, Brown Bear, What Do You See?* Rev. ed. New York: Henry Holt.

McGraw, Eloise Jarvis. 1961. *The Golden Goblet*. Rpt. ed. New York: Puffin.

Seuss, Theodor Geisel. 1957. *The Grinch That Stole Christmas*. New York: Random House Young Readers.

Weinberger, Kimberly. 2000. *Kids Rule*. New York: Mondo.

Wing, Natasha. 1996. *Jalapeño Bagels*. New York: Simon and Schuster Books for Young Children.

Bibliography

Anderson, Carl. 2000. *How's It Going? A Practical Guide for Conferring with Student Writers.* Portsmouth, NH: Heinemann.

Angelillo, Janet. 2002. *A Fresh Approach to Teaching Punctuation.* New York: Scholastic.

———. 2003. *Writing About Reading: From Book Talk to Literary Essays, Grades 3–8.* Portsmouth, NH: Heinemann.

Auman, Maureen. 2006. *Step Up to Writing.* 2d ed. Longmont, CA: Sporis West.

Calkins, Lucy McCormick. 1994. *The Art of Teaching Writing.* 3d ed. Portsmouth, NH: Heinemann.

Culham, Ruth. 2003. *6 +1 Traits of Writing.* New York: Scholastic.

———. 2005. *Using Picture Books to Teach Writing with the Traits: An Annotated Bibliography of More Than 200 Titles with Teacher-Tested Lessons.* New York: Scholastic.

Dole, Jan. 1997 (October). Public Education and Business Coalition Reading Comprehension workshop. Denver, Colorado.

Dorn, Linda, Cathy French, and Tammy Jones. 1998. *Apprenticeship in Literacy.* Portland, ME: Stenhouse.

Dorn, Linda, and Carla Soffos. 2001. *Scaffolding Young Writers: A Writers' Workshop Approach.* Portland, ME: Stenhouse.

Duke, J., and P. D. Pearson. 2002. "Effective Practices for Developing Reading Comprehension." In *What Research Has to Say About Reading Instruction*, edited by A. Farstrup and J. Samuels. Newark, DE: International Reading Association.

Duke, Nell K., and V. Susan Bennett-Armistead. 2003. *Reading and Writing Informational Text in the Primary Grades.* New York: Scholastic.

Farnan, Nancy, and Karin Dahl. 2003. "Children's Writing: Research and Practice." In *Handbook of Research on Teaching the English Language Arts*, edited by James Flood, Diane Lapp, James R. Squire, and Julie M. Jensen, 993–1007. Mahwah, NJ, and London: Lawrence Erlbaum.

Fielding, L., and P. D. Pearson. 1991. "Comprehension Instruction." In *Handbook of Reading Research*, vol. 2, edited by R. Barr, M. L. Kamil, P. B. Mosenthal, and P. D. Pearson, 815–60. New York: Longman.

Fisher, Doug, and Nancy Frey. 2003. "Writing Instruction for Struggling Adolescent Readers: A Gradual Release Model." *Journal of Adolescent and Adult Literacy* 46: 396–405.

Fletcher Ralph. 1993. *What a Writer Needs.* Portsmouth, NH: Heinemann.

———. 2001. *Nonfiction Craft Lessons.* Portland, ME: Stenhouse.

———. 2002. *Poetry Matters.* New York: Scholastic.

Flood, James, Diane Lapp, James R. Squire, Julie M. Jensen, eds. 2003. *Handbook of Research on Teaching the English Language Arts.* 2d ed. Sponsored by the International Reading Association and the National Council of Teachers of English. Mahwah, NJ, and London: Lawrence Erlbaum.

Fountas, Irene C., and Gay Su Pinnell. 2001. *Guiding Readers and Writers Grades 3–6: Teaching Comprehension, Genre, and Content Literacy.* Portsmouth, NH: Heinemann.

Freeman, Yvonne S., and David E. Freemann, with Sandra Mercuri. 2002. *Closing the Achievement Gap: How to Teach Limited-Formal-Schooling and Long-Term English Learners.* Portsmouth, NH: Heinemann.

Frey, Nancy, and Douglas Fisher. 2006. *Language Arts Workshop: Purposeful Reading and Writing Instruction.* Saddle River, NJ: Pearson Education.

Furr, D. 2003. "Struggling Readers Get Hooked on Writing." *The Reading Teacher* 56: 518–25.

Graves, Donald H., and Penny Kittle. 2005. *My Quick Writes for Inside Writing.* Portsmouth, NH: Heinemann.

Harvey, Stephanie. 1998. *Nonfiction Matters: Reading, Writing, and Research in Grades 3–8.* Portland, ME: Stenhouse.

Hoyt, Linda. 2002. *Make It Real: Strategies for Success with Informational Texts.* Portsmouth, NH: Heinemann.

———. 2003. "Linking Guided Reading and Guided Writing." In *Exploring Informational Texts: From Theory to Practice,* edited by Linda Hoyt, Margaret Mooney, and Brenda Parks. Portsmouth, NH: Heinemann.

Klein, Adria, Stanley Swartz, and Rebecca Shook. 2002. *Interactive Writing and Interactive Editing: Making Connections Between Writing and Reading.* Carlsbad, CA: Dominie.

Lamott, Anne. 1994. *Bird by Bird.* New York: Anchor.

Lane, Barry. 1999. *Reviser's Toolbox.* Shoreham, VT: Discover Writing Press.

Mariconda, Barbara. 1999. *The Most Wonderful Writing Lessons Ever.* New York: Scholastic.

———. 2001. *Step-by-Step Strategies for Teaching Expository Writing.* New York: Scholastic.

McCarrier, Andrea, Irene C. Fountas, and Gay Su Pinnell. 2000. *Interactive Writing: How Language and Literacy Come Together, K–2.* Portsmouth, NH: Heinemann.

Mooney, Margaret. 2003a. "Guided Writing." In *Exploring Informational Texts: From Theory to Practice,* edited by Linda Hoyt, Margaret Mooney, and Brenda Parks. Portsmouth, NH: Heinemann.

———. 2003b. "Thinking as a Reader and Writer of Informational Text." In *Exploring Informational Texts: From Theory to Practice,* edited by Linda Hoyt, Margaret Mooney, and Brenda Parks. Portsmouth, NH: Heinemann.

Northwest Regional Educational Laboratory. 1999. *Seeing with New Eyes: A Guide Book on Teaching and Assessing Writing.* Portland, OR: Northwest Regional Educational Laboratory.

Oczkus, Lori. 2003. *Reciprocal Teaching at Work: Strategies for Improving Reading Comprehension.* Newark, DE: International Reading Association.

———. 2004. *Super Six Comprehension Strategies: 35 Lessons and More for Reading Success.* Norwood, MA: Christopher Gordon.

Oczkus, Lori, Gery Baura, Kathy Murray, and Karen Berry. 2006. "Using the Love of 'Poitry' to Improve Primary Students' Writing." *The Reading Teacher* 59: 475–79.

Paley, Vivian. 2004. www.script.men.lu/documentation/archiv/decoprim/paley.htm. www.amshq.org/ams/vivian.html. www.ncte.org/elem/awards/educator/115530.htm-31k.

Persky, H. R., M. C. Daane, and Y. Yin. 2003. *The Nation's Report Card: Writing 2002.* 2002 NAEP Report. Washington, DC: U.S. Department of Education, Institute of Education Sciences, National Center for Education Statistics.

Randolf, Tina, and Eddie Garcia. 2005. *Guided Writing! Accelerate Your Students' Writing Skills.* San Diego, CA: Writing for Excellence.

Rasinski, Tim. 2003. *The Fluent Reader: Oral Reading Strategies for Building Word Recognition, Fluency, and Comprehension.* New York: Scholastic.

Ray, Katie Wood. 1999. *Wondrous Words: Writers and Writing in the Elementary Classroom.* Urbana, IL: National Council of Teachers of English.

Rief, Linda. 2003. *100 Quickwrites.* New York: Scholastic Teaching Resources.

Robb, Laura. 2004. *Nonfiction Writing: From the Inside Out.* New York: Scholastic.

Routman, Regie. 2000. *Kids' Poems: Teaching Children to Love Writing Poetry.* Separate volumes for kindergarten, grade 1, grade 2, and grades 3–4. New York: Scholastic.

———. 2005. *Writing Essentials: Raising Expectations and Results While Simplifying Teaching.* Portsmouth, NH: Heinemann.

Samway, Katherine Davies. 2006. *When English Language Learners Write: Connecting Research to Practice.* Portsmouth, NH: Heinemann.

Short, R. A., M. Kane, and T. Peeling, 2000. "Retooling the Reading Lesson: Matching the Right Tools to the Job." *The Reading Teacher* 54: 284–95.

Spandel, Vicki. 2001. *Books, Lessons, Ideas for Teaching the Six Traits: Writing in the Elementary and Middle Grades.* Wilmington, MA: Great Source.

———. 2003. *Creating Young Writers: Using the Six Traits to Enrich Writing Process in Primary Classrooms.* Boston: Pearson/Allyn and Bacon.

———. 2004. *Creating Writers Through Six-Trait Writing Assessment and Instruction.* 4th ed. Boston: Allyn and Bacon.

———. 2005. *The Nine Rights of Every Writer: A Guide for Teachers.* Portsmouth, NH: Heinemann.

Spivey, William. 1993. *Strengthening Student Writing.* Murietta, CA: Writing Express.

Stead, Tony. 2002. *Is That a Fact? Teaching Nonfiction Writing K–3.* Portland, ME: Stenhouse.

Sweeney, W. J., A. M. Ehrhardt, R. Gardner III, L. Jones, R. Greenfield, and S. Fribley. 1999. "Using Guided Notes with Academically at Risk High School Students During a Remedial Summer Social Studies Class." *Psychology in the Schools* 36: 305–18.

Thompkins, Gail, and Leah McGee. 1989. "Teaching Repetition as a Story Structure." In *Children's Comprehension of Text*, edited by Denise Muth. Newark, DE: International Reading Association.

Vgotsky, L. S. 1978. *Mind in Society: The Development of Higher Psychological Processes.* Edited by M. Cole, V. John-Steiner, and E. Souberman. Cambridge, MA: Harvard University Press.

Vogt, Mary Ellen. 1997. California Reading Association Meeting. "Read to Succeed" workshop. San Diego, CA.